CONTENTS

Background To The Marnoch Case   3

Marnoch Church   4

The Marnoch Case   4

The Intrusion At Marnoch   5

A New Church Needed   10

Opening Of The Church   19

The Disruption   20

The Free Church   22

New Marnoch Joins The Free Church   23

Other Places Of Free Church Worship In Marnoch   24

Marnoch Parish Church Schools   26

The Main Protagonists In Later Years   30

Reunion   39

FOREWORD

I will never forget the last regular service at Marnoch Old in January 1991. I felt as if the church was full of figures from the past - ministers, elders, beadles, organists, worshippers. I also remember hesitating in the pulpit for a long time after the benediction, feeling as if I was standing at the end of an era.

This book engendered similar feelings in me. Among its pages the characters of the past come alive again. Bob Peden takes us through the dramatic events which left their indelible mark on our Marnoch churches. If the reader was not familiar with the Marnoch story before, he or she will be in the picture after reading these pages.

The end of an era also marks the beginning of a new era. The past must be the springboard to the future. We owe it to all those whose story breathes through these pages, since their faithfulness in the past makes the future possible.

Our grateful thanks are due to Bob Peden, whose enthusiasm for this project seemed to grow as the amount of research multiplied. What could have been a chore seemed to be to him a joy. I hope that you too will catch something of his enthusiasm for his subject as you read.

Our churches were built to the glory of God. May He continue to be glorified as we move with Him from a fascinating past to an intriguing future.

Robert Jones

ACKNOWLEDGMENTS

Writing this brief history has been something of a voyage of discovery for me as, although I was aware of the rough outlines of the walkout at Marnoch in 1841, I knew nothing of the details of that and other events in the history of the churches involved. My voyage would not have been possible without the help of several institutions and individuals, whose help I am glad to acknowledge.

The basic source materials on the Marnoch churches were the church records provided by the Rev Bob Jones. Other sources in the form of newspapers and books were made available by the Northeast of Scotland Library Service HQ Local History Department and branch libraries at Aberchirder, Huntly and Macduff; Aberdeen University Library; and Aberdeen Central Library. Contacts and information were provided by Professor Stewart Brown, Department of History, New College, University of Edinburgh; Charles McKean; Professor George Peden, Department of History, University of Stirling; Dr David Walker, Chief Inspector of Historic Buildings, Historic Scotland; and the Scottish Record Office. Permission was kindly given by the National Library of Scotland to use the extracts from Ordnance Survey maps on pages 11 and 29, and by the British Library to use the illustrations on pages 33 and 34. Local people who provided contacts and information were John Barron, Mrs Sheena Bowie, Keith Brunskill, Peter and Keren Carter, Mrs Kathy Chalmers, William Davidson, Mrs Annie Hay, William Rennie, Mr & Mrs Clifford Sandison, Mrs Elspet Smith, Mrs Nellie Taylor, Mrs Laura Wilson and Mrs Phyllis Wright.

Special thanks are due to four people. Harry Mantell took great care over producing the superb original illustrations on the cover and title page, and on pages 6, 19, 27, 28, and 31. The Rev Bob Jones was always happy to provide advice and information throughout the project. Donald Graham and in particular my very understanding wife Alison also gave invaluable advice and undertook the tedious task of proof-reading.

Bob Peden

PARISH OF MARNOCH

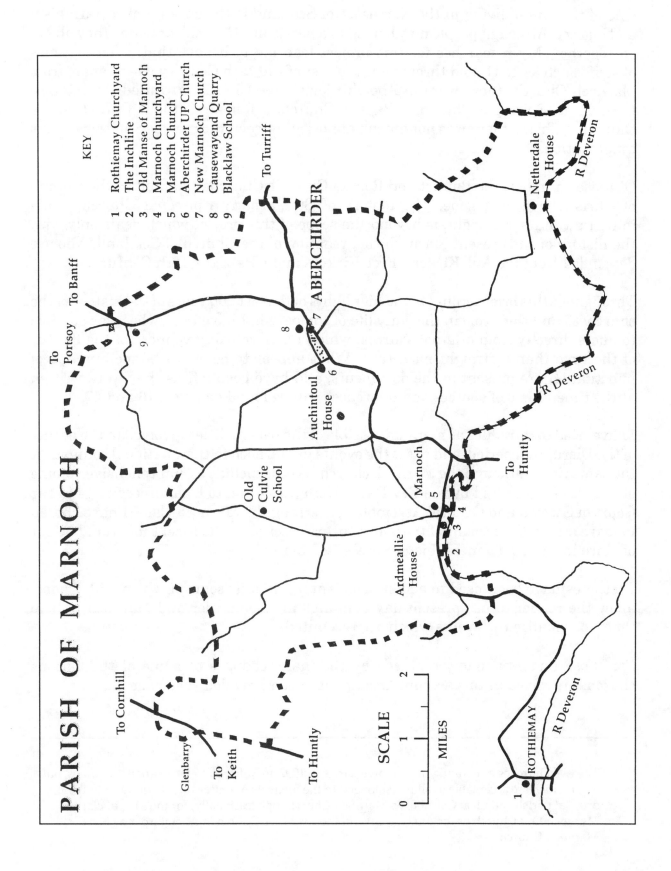

KEY

1 Rothiemay Churchyard
2 The Inchline
3 Old Manse of Marnoch
4 Marnoch Churchyard
5 Marnoch Church
6 Aberchirder UP Church
7 New Marnoch Church
8 Causewayend Quarry
9 Blacklaw School

ABERCHIRDER

To Turriff

To Banff

To Portsoy

To Cornhill

Glenbarry

To Keith

To Huntly

SCALE

0   1   2

MILES

Netherdale House

R Deveron

R Deveron

To Huntly

Auchintoul House

Old Culvie School

Marnoch

Ardmeallie House

ROTHIEMAY

R Deveron

1

AUTHOR'S NOTE

One of the joys of living in the Northeast of Scotland is the absence of sectarianism and bigotry. Although people may belong to a particular Church - or none - they all get on together. My researches for this project lead me to believe that, even at times of strife such as 1841, and throughout the rest of the 19th Century when, apart from Marnoch Church, there were in Aberchirder a Free Church, a United Prebyterian Church, an Episcopal Church, a Baptist Church, a Roman Catholic Church and a Church of Christ, there was not much animosity between the members of the various congregations.

Of these churches, the Baptist and Roman Catholic Churches, as well as the Church of Christ, have long gone. The history of St Marnan's Episcopal Church, while important in its own right, is beyond the scope of this project which deals only with the history of the present Marnoch congregation of the Church of Scotland, who are descended from the Aul' Kirkers, Free Kirkers and UPs of the 19th Century.

Throughout this brief account of the highlights of the last 200 years of the history of the churches* and their role in the daily life of the parish, I have tried wherever possible to quote directly from original sources, which I believe will give more of the flavour of the time than a straight narrative. (What appear to be errors of spelling and of punctuation are present in the documents, and have been left as they were written at the time.) Lists of sources and references will be found on pages 46 and 47.

I have tried to introduce as many as possible of the personalities involved in the events of the Disruption period, and to set the events in Marnoch in their national context. At the same time, although the Marnoch church records include a comprehensive volume of documents collected by the Rev David Henry, relating to legal proceedings in the Court of Session and General Assembly concerning the Marnoch Case, I have chosen to leave a detailed account of these to a future researcher, as I feel they would be out of place in the brief general history presented here.

Footnotes have been used to add supplementary details, some of which will, I hope, allow the reader to use present-day buildings in Aberchirder and Marnoch to help them to visualise the events which are recounted.

For those understandably confused by the many changes of name of the various churches involved in this account, a chart has been provided - see page 43.

---

*   The two churches celebrating their anniversaries in 1992 are referred to by a variety of names, not all of which are acceptable to all parishioners! In the interests of uniformity, I will refer to the original parish church at Cairnhill as **Marnoch Church** (or occasionally, for the sake of clarity, **Marnoch Old Church** or **the old church**) and the 1842 Free Church in Aberchirder as **New Marnoch Church**.

BACKGROUND TO THE MARNOCH CASE

In the 2000 years of its history, Christianity has seen many arguments and splits over matters of doctrine, form of service, style of Church government and so on. In the Church of Scotland in the early 19th Century a great split took place over the issues of who should have the final say in the appointment of ministers, and what the relationship between Church and state should be.

This split - the Disruption - had its origins in the Patronage Act of 1712, which the newly formed British Parliament passed to bring Scotland into line with England, giving the local landowner the right to appoint a minister regardless of the wishes of the congregation. This Act was unpopular with many Scots, for whom union with England was seen as a sellout by the landowning and business classes for personal gain. The idea of patronage also ran counter to ideas of democracy, spread by radical politicians, which gained increasing support in the first half of the 19th Century. Already in the 18th Century various secessions had taken place, and by 1773 there were reckoned to be 180 congregations outside the Established Church of Scotland.

By the 1830s the Church of Scotland had become divided into two camps - the Moderates, who accepted the idea of patronage, and the Evangelicals, who believed the congregation should have the final say in appointing a minister. Evangelicals also believed that there was a need for spiritual revival in the Church, and that many ministers were not giving their congregations meaningful religious teaching.

The Evangelicals persuaded the General Assembly of 1834 to pass a Veto Act, which allowed the congregation to veto (forbid) the intrusion of a minister by a patron against their will. This ecclesiastical Act, of course, contradicted the secular Patronage Act.

The first patron to challenge the Veto Act was Lord Kinnoul in Auchterarder, and he won a victory in the Court of Session in 1837. Two years later a case regarding the parish of Lethendy involved the Presbytery of Dunkeld and the Court of Session. But, of 150 vacancies between 1834 and 1839, 140 were settled harmoniously, because patrons followed the wishes of their congregations. [1]

The third dispute over the Veto Act concerned Marnoch, and it was to lead to the setting up of the first Free Church in Scotland.

MARNOCH CHURCH

While New Marnoch Church celebrates its 150th anniversary, the present Marnoch Old Church celebrates its 200th. Originally the church had been beside the churchyard on the banks of the Deveron.* But in 1791 the patron and heritors, having decided that the old church was

> totally ruinous & inadequate for accommodating the people in the Parish, they were of the opinion, that the building of a new one at the back of the Old Church would occasion digging very deep for foundations, disturb severall of the graves, & very much hamper the burying ground which is already much confined, & they therefore were of the opinion that the proper stance for the new Church would be at Cairnhill. [2]

When the new building was ready in 1792 the Presbytery

> approved of the choice of building a church there, in regard it is on a dry eminence, where the sound of the Bell will be heard much better than where it was formerly & ...not in the least liable to the hurtful air that frequently arises from the burying grounds... [3]

However, when the interior of the church was inspected, the Presbytery found that

> the pulpit seemed evidently to be too low, & it was necessary to raise it at least Eighteen inches or two feet, in order that the people in the back Galleries might hear and see the minister... [4]

This, and many other minor details, were duly altered and the new church was then ready for use.

THE MARNOCH CASE

In 1837 the Rev William Stronach of Marnoch died. The patrons, the trustees of the Earl of Fife, presented the Rev John Edwards, a schoolmaster at Cairnie, for the vacancy. Mr Edwards had previously been dismissed by Mr Stronach at the request of the majority of the male communicants.** The congregation now wanted the Rev David Henry, Mr Stronach's assistant in his last years, to be appointed. The patrons then accepted the congregation's wishes, and nominated Mr Henry instead.

The Rev Edwards refused to accept this decision, and took legal action to have it reversed. This began a titanic struggle which, for six years, set Moderates against Evangelicals, split the Presbytery of Strathbogie, and led to the setting up of New Marnoch Church, which celebrates its 150th anniversary in 1992.

---

*   See map on page 11.

**   Mr Edwards did his daily duties in the school, and on Saturday evening or Sunday morning drove to Marnoch and preached in the Church. This arrangement was not found very convenient by the people, as Mr Edwards being unordained, could not dispense the communion or baptise or officiate at a marriage. Moreover, his pulpit ministrations were not acceptable to the people. [5]

THE INTRUSION AT MARNOCH

For the Marnoch congregation, matters came to a head early in 1841. A majority of members of Strathbogie Presbytery had supported the Rev Edwards in his legal battle, and had been suspended by the Church.* But they insisted that they represented the Presbytery, and were intent on appointing Mr Edwards. On 3 January 1841 Mr Walker (the suspended minister of Huntly) demanded the key to Marnoch church from Mr Henry, and opened the church.

> Old Sandy Mackintosh, the beadle, by refusing to give the use of the Church Bible to the preacher, produced not a little excitement. [However, at Mr Henry's request] the Bible was returned to the pulpit, and, giving up the church to Mr Walker...[the Rev Henry] proceeded to Cairnhill, a farm in the vicinity, where, in the open court-yard, in the midst of a snowstorm, the parishioners of Marnoch gathered round him while he conducted the usual services. [6]

The *Witness*, a pro-Evangelical Edinburgh newspaper, reckoned that Mr Henry's outdoor congregation had been 1100-1200, while only about 40 had remained in the church.** It went on to report the rest of the day's events:

> Mr Henry preached again in the evening in the empty factory*** in the village of Aberchirder, which has been used for some time as a temporary preaching station, and the accommodation of which the parishioners enjoy free, by the kindness of Wm Aitken Esq of Auchintoul. It was ascertained that there would not have been fewer than 700 in this house, and about the stairs and windows, and many went away without being able to get within hearing. Thus passed the first Sabbath of 1841 in the parish of Marnoch. [7]

On Thursday 21 January five of the suspended members of Strathbogie Presbytery turned up at Marnoch Church to induct Mr Edwards. In the *Aberdeen Banner* of 23 January the editor, Alexander Troup, in a fiercely anti-intrusionist account, devoted over 12 000 words to the amazing events of the day. The following extracts give a good idea of what happened - albeit from a partisan point of view:

---

* Mr Edwards had raised an action in the Court of Session to have it declared that the Presbytery were bound to take him on trials. In 1838 the Presbytery, by a majority, voted to recognise the authority of the Court of Session, and to do nothing till the legal action was settled. In 1839, the General Assembly censured the Presbytery for accepting the Court of Session's authority and banned them from taking any steps towards the induction of Mr Edwards. A fortnight later the Court of Session ruled that the Presbytery must proceed to settle Mr Edwards on the parish, which a majority of the Presbytery agreed to do. For this these seven Strathbogie ministers were suspended by the Assembly in December 1839. [8]

** James Wilson, Cots of Netherdale, was inside the church, and recorded that
Mr Walker...preached...from Jeremiah xxviii 15, last clause of the verse - "The Lord hath not sent thee" (an unfortunate text for a friend of Edwards to choose)...There were present three heads of families viz Peter Taylor, Peter Findlater, both in Aberchirder, and John Lawrence, Mill of Netherdale, some strangers (incl 3 lawyers), some intrusionists from other parishes - his congregation amounting in all to 85...At which time...Rev D Henry...preached...at Cairnhill Farmyard...from 1st Timothy 15. [9]

*** See footnote * on page 12.

INTRUSION OF MR EDWARDS
UPON THE PEOPLE OF MARNOCH

Thursday the 21st January, 1841, will continue a memorable day in the annals of the Church of Scotland...The intrusion of Mr Edwards into Marnoch...from the opposition alike of patron, of people, and of the Assembly, is without parallel in the history of Scotland, or Scotland's Church. Very great and solemn interest has been taken in this matter, and we believe it was the intention of a considerable number of gentlemen, from Aberdeen, to have been present at Marnoch on the day in question; but, on Tuesday afternoon and evening, a very heavy snow storm came on...and, by Wednesday morning, it was evident that [the roads] would be in many parts impassable.

The *Earl of Fife* coach was, we believe, the only one that left town for the north by any of the high roads on Wednesday morning. From the admirable arrangements of the proprietors of that coach, their passengers reached Turriff early in the afternoon. At Turriff, there were still eight miles of a cross road to traverse to Aberchirder, and three farther to the Church of Marnoch. The state of this road may be gathered from the fact that a carriage, with four horses, was several hours in reaching the village and was brought to a complete stand at five different places.

PROCEEDINGS OF THE MORNING

Early in the morning of Thursday, [people] were seen in little companies from every quarter, with some stout man leading the way...By ten o'clock vast numbers had collected about the Manse of Marnoch, and on to eleven large parties continued to

THE OLD MANSE OF MARNOCH

6

assemble...The principal actors in the day's calamity arrived in two or three carriages ...and, we believe, it was with considerable difficulty that they forced their way through the snow to force on this settlement...

Shortly after 11, the very small party of Intrusionists, along with Mr Edwards, moved from the Manse to the Church...The key was at once given to them. Some difficulty arose from the vast crowd assembled at the Church door...in procuring a passage through it; but this was effected by Mr Duncan of Aberdeen, the [legal] agent for the parishioners and the elders. Mr Duncan, before entering the Church, informed the people that it had been agreed that the lower part of the building should be set apart for the parishioners, and that strangers would be admitted to the galleries, which were immediately and densely filled, although only a small portion of the people assembled obtained admission. Shortly after Mr Edwards and his friends had entered, it became apparent that one of the beams which supports the gallery was giving way; and the front of the first seats was pressed out by the dense mass of individuals leaning forward upon it. The alarm was very rapidly spread, and a rush was made from the gallery by both doors...When order had been restored, Mr Stronach of Ardmeallie addressed the assemblage from the pulpit stairs - reminded them that...if they only kept their seats, there could be no danger...

Mr Thomson of Keith opened the proceedings by prayer...At the close of the prayer, Mr Murray, Mains of Pittendreich, one of the elders, said "I wish to ask you, by whose authority have you met here?"

Mr Thomson of Keith - By the authority of the National Church, and in the name of the Lord Jesus Christ.

...By this time the greater part of the crowd, who remained through the whole day about the Church, had assembled, either within or without doors, and we should think the number is not over-estimated at two thousand.

There then followed an argument between Mr Cruickshank, Clerk to the Presbytery, and Mr Duncan. Mr Cruickshank refused to hear Mr Duncan's statement until he had presented his authority, and Mr Duncan refused to do this as he did not recognise the suspended ministers as representing the Presbytery of Strathbogie. But eventually Mr Duncan was allowed to read the protest of the elders and heads of families against the intrusion of Mr Edwards, which read, in part:

'We, the Subscribers, Elders, Heads of Families and other Parishioners of Marnoch, do hereby intimate to you, Messrs Walker, Cruickshank Jun., Thomson, Masson, Cowie, who have come here for the avowed purpose of inducting and ordaining Mr John Edwards as minister of the said parish, that any such act or proceeding is illegal and unconstitutional, in respect you have been suspended by the Supreme Ecclesiastical Court from the exercise of all ecclesiastical functions, and have been specially interdicted and prohibited from taking any steps whatever in the settlement of Mr Edwards...

We maintain that Mr Edwards can have no charge in the parish of Marnoch, for his call is signed but by one communicant *...We have but one alternative left. We must and shall, united, leave the Church and seek ministrations elsewhere. And to you, and to Mr Edwards, shall we attribute an expulsion from that building which we and our fathers have hitherto frequented, and which we fondly desired to frequent till death.'

(This document was signed by five elders and over 450 communicants.)

---

*   This was Peter Taylor, an Aberchirder innkeeper, referred to on page 5.

DEPARTURE OF THE PARISHIONERS OF MARNOCH FROM THE CHURCH

Having read the protests, Mr DUNCAN said - As agent for the elders, male heads of families and communicants of Marnoch, I have now only to say that they take no further part in these unconstitutional proceedings...and leave you to force a minister on the parish against the people's will.
(*Great cheering.*) The people of Marnoch immediately arose from their seats in the body of the church, and left the house where they and their fathers had long worshipped, in silence, and many doubtless in sorrow...Old men with heads as white as the snow that lay deep on their native hills, the middle aged, and the young... joined together in this solemn protest...

THE PARISHIONERS LEAVE MARNOCH CHURCH *

They literally went out into the wilderness, for they have no Church in the meantime to which they shall turn. They went out, many in tears, and all in grief. We noticed some very aged men, who may not live to return in joy, who literally wept as they passed over the threshold of *their* church...

The suspended ministers then proceeded with the induction of Mr Edwards, to much heckling from the spectators who, of course, still included opponents of the intrusion from Marnoch and other parishes:

We meet here as consitutional members of the Church of Scotland - (*hisses*) - in the name of the Lord Jesus Christ - (*cries of No, no; Oh, oh; in the name of the Court of Session*) - to judge honourably, honestly, and fearlessly of any special objections that might be brought againt the presentee. The people of Marnoch have not thought fit to recognise us. We shall still proceed to act in our belief in strict accordance with the rules of our National Church - (*cries of Against the orders of the Church*) - and instruct our officer - (*great noise*) - to proceed to the...door of the Church, and read the following intimation - (*hisses*).

---

*   From Brown, *Annals of the Disruption*. The artist does not seem to have visited the scene of the events, as the building and background do not correspond to reality!

The intimation called on all 'Elders, communicants, or parishioners of Marnoch, to state any objections...why Mr John Edwards, presentee to the parish, should not now be admitted as Minister of the parish, and inducted into the Church of Marnoch'. (*Great hissing.*)...

SCENE NEAR THE CHURCHYARD OF MARNOCH

When the parishioners left the church, they proceeded in a body to the foot of the hill on which their church is built, and where the roads leading to Aberchirder, Ardmellie, and the Manse separate. There, in a little hollow, they held their first meeting after this virtual expulsion from their church. Mr Duncan...addressed a few words to them [after which] the parishioners separated, and in a few minutes they were seen hastening homewards in their different directions.

RIOTOUS PROCEEDINGS IN THE CHURCH

When we returned to the Church, we were informed that within doors there had been a considerable amount of noise, and such missiles as snow-balls had been flung at the Intrusionists. Mr Thomson of Keith had attempted to make his way to the pulpit to commence the service, but...had been obstructed; and when we entered the Church, several people were employed in throwing snow, pieces of bread and, Mr Walker of Huntly said, copper-coins, at the Intrusionists, who occupied the pew on the right of the pulpit, and certainly looked as in a most distressing plight.*
Mr Stronach of Ardmeallie was then observed riding up to the Church. On entering, he said he had been sent for to quell a riot, but he saw none...
MR WALKER - As a member of this Presbytery, I call on Captain Anderson to obtain peace, and do his duty...
MR STRONACH - Captain Anderson, give me two of your men to clear the passes. Now mark me, men, you are to do so in the gentlest manner. You have no right to strike or act roughly...
Mr Stronach contrived to clear one pass and the policemen the other without the slightest unpleasant occurrence, the people gradually falling into their seats.
MR STRONACH - ...Mr Thomson, there is now perfect quiet, so you had better proceed, and be as short and concise as you possibly can. (*Laughter.*)

Mr Edwards was then ordained, and Mr Troup concluded his report with these comments:
...Until Thursday, we never saw a minister ordained, and have no single parishioner, no human being in his charge, to bid him God-speed, and pray for his well-being. So it was with pitiable Mr Edwards. True, Mr Peterkin [the advocate hired by the suspended ministers] wished him much joy - a cautious clever gentleman - thinking of his long bill - and Mr Robertson of the *Constitutional* [a pro-Moderate newspaper] shook hands with him warmly...And Captain Anderson of the Police took his arm... while two or three policemen surrounded him, and the people *hissed, hissed, hissed* a minister from his church door on his ordination day! We never saw a presentee so wretched that he was utterly friendless! [10]

---

* Mr Clifford Sandison recalls being told that his greatgrandfather, who was present, insisted that all the trouble that day was caused by the "UPs" from the parish and elsewhere. [11] As the UP Church was not founded till 1847, this must refer to members of the United Secession Church in Aberchirder and members of other secession churches in other parishes (see pages 3 and 39).

A more typical editorial response to the events at Marnoch came from the *Glasgow Herald*, which said

> ...We most deeply regret that the Church should have...put herself in a state of antagonism to the civil authority, from which alone the present difficulties have arisen. The repeal of the veto act, when declared illegal, would have prevented a world of evil...If we look back for only a few years, we find the Patrons vying with the Presbyteries in their anxiety to consult the wishes of the people. All was proceeding most...happily, when the Church, in an evil hour, usurped the province of legislation and determined to maintain her right to legislate in the face of the state...[12]

The *Aberdeen Journal* also had some caustic comments to make about the *Banner* account of the walkout - see page 30.

(The problems of the suspended ministers continued after the walkout. They applied to the Court of Session for their ban by the General Assembly to be lifted, and got a decree in their favour. The Church then put them on trial, and they were deposed from the office of the ministry at the Assembly in May 1841.)

A NEW CHURCH NEEDED

The members of the congregation who had walked out now had the problem of finding new premises for worship. On 25 January the heads of families held a meeting in Aberchirder. From the minute book of this and subsequent meetings, we can follow the steps to the opening of New Marnoch Church on 1 March 1842.

> Aberchirder 25 Jan 1841
> ...to arrange for obtaining temporary stations for the worship of God in the parish and to consider the proprety of erecting a new church and manse in the parish.
> Mr Murray, Mains of Netherdale, was unanimously called to the chair.
> The meeting was opened with prayer by the Rev D Henry. It was then proposed that a preaching station should be opened at the Inchline* on the premises of Mr Geo Harper** and agreed to - and that worship should be maintained at Aberchirder as

---

*   See map on page 11. The location of these premises is described as being in a beautiful wooded dell about half a mile from the Parish Church.[13] Although there is some doubt as to the exact location, the late Jimmy Reid, who lived in the area, is quoted as confirming it was on the flat piece of ground by the riverside, reached by a track branching off the Rothiemay road a quarter of a mile west of Old Manse of Marnoch.

**   A letter to Rev Henry signed by George Harper and five others reads:
>   Brae of Ardmeallie, 23 Jany. 1841
> Revd Sir,
> Owing to the situation in which we are now placed by the intrusion of Mr Edwards into this Parish as temporary places of worship we consider ar necessary at present we ar anxous if you thought proper to erect one in this corner of the Parish. We see that Wrights Shop at Saw Mill belonging to Geo. Harper would hold from 150 to 160 people with little expense or trouble and could be ready before Sabbath the 31st and if necessary an addition could easily be added please send an answer as soon as convenient...[14]

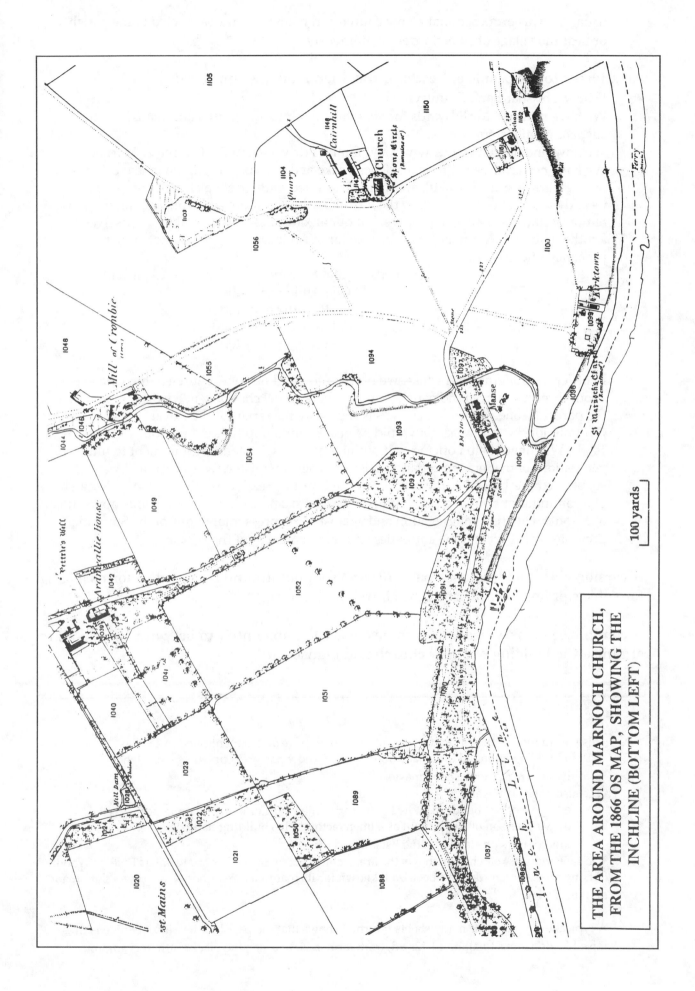

THE AREA AROUND MARNOCH CHURCH, FROM THE 1866 OS MAP, SHOWING THE INCHLINE (BOTTOM LEFT)

100 yards

11

usual *. It was proposed that a new church and manse should be erected in the parish at or near the village of Aberchirder, unanimously agreed to. [15]

An address to the people of Scotland was then read and approved:

Fellow Christians and Countrymen,

We have now had Mr Edwards forcibly intruded into our church and manse by the suspended ministers...

We now find ourselves, our wives and families driven from the Church of Marnoch... We have been compelled for conscience's sake and the sake of religion to leave - with our hearts sad and sorrowful, and our spirits filled with grief - a church once free to us and ours but now given up to the intruder...We are at present worshipping in such tempory stations as we can procure, but our anxious desire is to build for ourselves another church at Marnoch, and a manse for our minister, and to promote other parochial interests...

	(Signed)	John Murray	Elder	Chairman
		Geo Anderson	Elder	
		Jas Robertson	Elder	
		A Innes	Elder	
		Wm Allan	Elder	

In order to strengthen our cause, we propose to build our new church at the village about three miles from the parish church, where a new church is needed even though the parochial one was open to us - as is shown by the report of the Royal Commissioners - and where it would be needed for a population for about 1300 or 1400... We cannot help noticing that our new church will stand a monument to future generations of that era in Scotland's History when a minister...was intruded by a suspended presbytery, at the bidding of the Court of Session, on the strength of a call by one communicant out of a population of 2800, and against the...conscientious opposition of a united christian congregation and against the express injunctions of the Supreme Ecclesiastical court and the entreaties and remonstrances of the patron.** [16]

A version of this address (see page 13) was sent out around Scotland on forms asking for subscriptions towards the new church and manse.**

A committee of sixty heads of families was then appointed to act with the elders to organise the building of a new church and manse.

---

* This would refer to the empty factory referred to on page 5. It is mentioned in 1870 as
> a building intended for a hand-loom factory (now partly occupied as a residence by the Free Church schoolmaster) [17]

- see also pages 19, 26 and 27 - and in 1891 as
> a large block of building...now belonging to the Hall Company...having been erected by Mr Morison of Auchintoul as a linen factory. This building had been used as a kind of mission station by the Established Church. [18]

The 1866 map of Aberchirder shows the area behind the present Memorial Hall as Factory Wood. (At one time Aberchirder had been well known for its manufacture of heavy winceys - cloth made of linen and wool.) [19]

** A typical example of the many sheets returned shows that the parish of Lesslie, Aberdeenshire, raised 39 donations totalling £1 12s 6d, from farmers, labourers, the blacksmith, servants, etc. [20]

ADDRESS

FROM THE

PARISHIONERS OF MARNOCH.

At a MEETING OF HEADS OF FAMILIES in the Parish of Marnoch, held at Aberchirder, on 25th January 1841—Mr MURRAY, Farmer, Mains of Netherdale, one of the Elders, in the Chair—the following ADDRESS TO THE CHRISTIAN PEOPLE OF SCOTLAND was agreed to :—

FELLOW-CHRISTIANS AND COUNTRYMEN,—We have now had Mr Edwards forcibly intruded into our Church and Manse by the suspended Ministers. The circumstances of our case must be as well known to you as they have been painful to us. Mr Edwards was assistant to our late respected minister, Mr Stronach, for three years. His services were so unedifying, and the opposition to him was so strong in the parish, that he was removed from that situation about a year before Mr Stronach's death. He, however, received the presentation from the aged gentleman who at that time was patron—in ignorance, we believe, of the opinions of the parishioners respecting him. His call was signed by but ONE communicant out of a population of 2800, while 261 heads of families, communicants (out of a roll of 300), dissented from his settlement. After a protracted litigation, accompanied with much expense and trouble to us, he was rejected by the Presbytery in obedience to the orders of the General Assembly. A majority of the Presbytery of Strathbogie afterwards sustained his call and prescribed his trials. We *then* appeared and offered special objections, signed by more of our number than the dissent was. The majority of the Presbytery would neither allow us to state nor prove them, nor would they receive our protest. For their disobedience to the Church, and their oppressive conduct towards us, they were suspended ; but, nevertheless, in our absence, and in the knowledge that we had offered objections perfectly distinct from the Veto law, they found Mr Edwards qualified. Then, as if in perfect mockery of justice, they publish their edicts, calling upon us to state our objections, *when* they were, of course, prepared to reject them as irrelevant, because they had already found Mr Edwards qualified,—and when they had placed themselves in a situation, which, they well knew, precluded us from recognising them as judges.

On the day of the pretended settlement, we attended, entered our solemn protest, and quietly withdrew from the church.

We hope that our conduct throughout this long and distressing conflict has been characterized by Christian patience and forbearance, and such as to recommend our necessitous circumstances to the sympathies of our Christian countrymen.

We now find ourselves, our wives, and families, driven from the church of Marnoch, where we and our fathers have worshipped, and where we desire to continue to worship until our death. We have been compelled for conscience' sake and the sake of religion, to leave—with our hearts sad and sorrowful, and our spirits filled with grief—a church once free to us and ours, but now given up to the intruder. " Our Zion is indeed a wilderness—our *holy* house where our fathers praised the Lord," if not " burned up," is barred against us. But we are of good courage—our trust is in the Lord our God, the Holy One of Israel, our Saviour, who hath said to his people—" When thou passest through the waters, I will be with thee ; and through the rivers, they shall not overflow thee ; when thou walkest through the fire thou shalt not be burned, neither shall the flame kindle upon thee."

We are at present worshipping in such temporary stations as we can procure ; but our anxious desire is, to build for ourselves another church in Marnoch, and a manse for our minister, and to promote other parochial interests. To forward these objects for the glory of God and the spiritual interests of this large and populous parish, we rely upon the countenance and support of the Supreme Ecclesiastical Assembly of our Church, and we appeal to the sympathies of our Christian countrymen. And as you value the cause in which we have suffered so much, so may your sympathy for our position and our feelings be manifested in favour of this application. And may the Lord repay you manifold.——(Signed) JOHN MURRAY, Elder, *Chairman ;* GEORGE ANDREW, Elder ; JAMES ROBERTSON, Elder ; ALEXANDER INNES, Elder ; WILLIAM ALLAN, Elder.——*Marnoch,* 25th January 1841.

*** A Committee, consisting of about forty heads of families, communicants, from all corners of the parish, was appointed to act along with the Session in this matter.

We propose to build our new Church at the village, about three miles from the parish church, *where a new church is needed* even though the parochial one was open to us—as is shewn by the report of the Royal Commissioners—and where it will be needed for a population of about 1300 or 1400 *when* the parish church is again opened up to us—which we hope will be at no very distant day. We cannot help noticing, that our new church will stand a monument (and we hope the only monument) to future generations, of that era in Scotland's history, when a minister (and we earnestly hope but one) was intruded by a suspended Presbytery, at the bidding of the Court of Session, on the strength of a call by one communicant out of a population of 2800, and against the strenuous and conscientious opposition of a united Christian congregation, and against the express injunctions of the Supreme Ecclesiastical Court, and the entreaties and remonstrances of the patron,—and when the worldly ambition and temporal interests of one man were deemed of greater importance than the concientious feelings and spiritual interests of a whole parish,—and when the spiritual instruction of the people was held to be secondary to the appointment of a licentiate to fill the benefice.

This paper to be returned, with any Subscriptions, to Robert Paul, Esq., Commercial Bank, as soon as possible.

	£	s.	d.		£	s.
William Sorley	1			R B Kinnear (Spott) 1	7	7
Waugh	1			A Spence		5
Green	1					
	1				8	13
	1					

At the next meeting, on 15 February, it was decided that a church of about 900 sittings would be required. A committee of fifteen was appointed to look for a suitable site. Several letters of support for the congregation from other parts of Scotland - and England - were read to the meeting.*

On 22 February, the next meeting was held. Mr Stronach of Ardmeallie was in correspondence with Mr Aitken of Auchintoul for a site, which the committee was empowered to buy. More letters of support from other parishes were read.

At the meeting of 15 March it was announced that agreement had been reached with Mr Aitken, who was willing to give off in feu

> ...a piece of ground on the market place of Aberchirder consisting of one hundred and twenty falls Scotch measure...at least ninety falls west of the angle ground betwixt the road from Banff to Huntly and the road leading to the middle of the village...**
> The feuars are to have the right to take materials for building the Church and manse from the quarry on that part of the Estate of Auchintoul called Corskie***. The value

---

* The following examples [21] are typical of the many letters received by the Rev Henry:

31 Jan 1841

Living as we do, in your immediate neighbourhood, we have been witnesses of the troubles and anxieties, to which for the sake of religion and conscience you have been exposed. We desire to tender to you...our sincere and hearty sympathy. In all that has befallen you, we would recognise the hand of the Lord, who...in his sovereignty has made you to suffer, while others have been exempted...

Joseph Thorburn,
Minister of Forglen
(and elders)

4 Feb 1841

...When you have finally resolved as to what you are to do about a new Church and should you stand in need of aid - may I request that you would let me know and then my parish will consider it an honor to be allowed to contribute a small sum to promote the comfort and edification of men who have suffered so severely and yet conducted themselves so admirably...

Francis Gillies
Minister of Rattray Parish

6 Feb 1841

...You will, before this, have received the *Scottish Guardian*, containing an account of the Meeting held in Glasgow, on the evening of Monday last, to sympathise with the good people of Marnoch in their present trying circumstances...The subscription in Glasgow to assist in the erection of a new Church in Marnoch is getting on well. It now exceeds £300...I have such small sums as sixpence sent to me...from the poorer classes who have but little to give...

William Collins, Glasgow

11 Feb 1841

...I do most heartily applaud your whole conduct as having been characterised throughout by Christian wisdom and forbearance...I shall feel highly honoured and delighted to be of the smallest service to you...

John Thomson
Minister of Mariners Church, Leith

** Now the 'Point'.

*** This is presumably Causewayend Quarry [22]

of the materials so taken to be paid for by Mr Aitken...

Mr Henry individually agrees to rent from Mr Aitken the angle ground on the east of the said fued ground, and also the ground immediately west of the said fued ground extending to John Browns Acre...

...Mr Aitken is to have the privilege of holding the first Aberchirder Market on or about the Sixteenth Current on the ground as formerly, and thereafter the market is to be changed to the square of the village.*

A week later, on 22 March, a plan was submitted from James Raeburn, Architect, Edinburgh (who later designed Trinity & Alvah Church in Banff - described by McKean[23] as "unusually classical for a Free Church").** The plans were in general approved of, though some alterations were made. Mr John Duncan of Aberdeen (who had acted for the elders on the day of the walkout) was to be asked to obtain a charter or lease for the site from Mr Aitken.

A body of trustees and managers*** was then appointed to

have the management of all the funds - the power of laying out the ground - entering into contracts for the erection of the buildings - conducting the work untill finished, apportioning the seats and seat rents - assembling and consulting the committee of Heads of Families when they think desirable...[24]

The trustees and managers at their next meeting on 8 April were shown plans and specifications from Mr Raeburn, which were thought to be too expensive. But it was felt only fair to him to submit the plans to contractors without alterations to see if they could do the job within the limit of the £1200 available, and to try to reduce the cost the committee drew up a list of changes which would still retain the overall appearance of the building. Mr Raeburn would be asked to attend on the day of contract. It was

---

*   The present Market Park appears on the 1st Edition OS Map of 1866, so the market must have moved there from the Square between 1842 and 1866.

** Mr Raeburn had been in correspondence with the Rev R S Candlish of St George's Church Edinburgh, a leading Evangelical, on 1 February 1841:
    Reverend Sir,
    Understanding that the funds of the Church propose to build a New place of worship, for the benefit of that most respectable, but ill-used people the parishioners of Marnoch...I beg respectfully to offer my professional services if they can be of any use in aiding a good cause by making Plans, Specifications, and giving all directions...Should my offer be accepted...I shall take pleasure in visiting the Site of the proposed New Church at my own expense so as not to encroach on the funds set apart for the New Building...
    I am
    Reverend Sir
    Sincerely Yours
    James Raeburn
    Architect

    Just before the meeting on 22 March, a letter was received from Dalmahoy & Wood (agents of the nonintrusion committee in Edinburgh):
    ...We have sent the plans for the new Church at Marnoch in a parcel by coach...You will find a letter from Mr Raeburn along with the plans, from which you will see that he estimates the expense at £1200, and not at £1500, as we mentioned in our letter to you; but before everything was completed we think it would cost the latter sum. [25]

*** See page 18.

15

resolved to advertise for contractors in the Aberdeen newspapers, estimates to be in by Thursday 13 April at Mrs Allan's Inn (as the Fife Arms Hotel was known at that time):

DAY OF CONTRACT FIXED.

Contractors are Wanted.

FOR Executing the MASON, WRIGHT, PLASTER, SLATER, and PLUMBER Work of a New CHURCH and MANSE, at ABERCHIRDER.

The Plans and Specifications for the Church may be seen on application to Mr WM. ALLAN, Merchant; or Mr WM. CUMMING, Postmaster, Aberchirder; with either of whom sealed offers for any part, or the whole of the work, may be lodged; before, or on Thursday 15th curt., at 12 o'clock noon, when the Trustees are to meet in Mrs ALLAN'S INN, Aberchirder, and contract for the work, if satisfactory offers are made.

It is expected that, before the above day, the Plans and Specifications for the Manse will be ready, and that a contract for the same will be entered into at the sametime.

The Trustees do not bind themselves to accept the lowest offers, unless in all respects satisfactory.

Aberchirder, 8th April, 1841.

26

The trustees and managers met again on 12 April. Mr Henry laid before the meeting measurements of mason and wright work supplied from Mr Raeburn's plans by Mr George Cousin, ordained surveyor, Edinburgh. Revised specifications as proposed by the previous meeting had been drawn up by Mr William Milne, mason, Aberchirder, to be submitted to the contractors along with Mr Raeburn's originals.

The following week, on 15 April, the trustees and managers met with Messrs Raeburn and Milne as the sealed offers from contractors were opened. Even with the altered specifications, they were too expensive. So Mr Raeburn was thanked for his efforts, and it was decided to find other plans - a job deputed to the Rev Henry and Mr Milne, to be done within eight days! The contractors who had already submitted bids were informed of this, and told that the plans should be put on display for a day in Aberdeen and on 26 and 27 April in Aberchirder. Contracts for the manse would also be sought by public advertisement.

On 28 April the Rev Henry submitted plans for a church from James Henderson, Builder & Architect, Aberdeen*, which had been supplied free of charge. Sealed offers were then opened, and contracts were signed immediately. These can be summarised as follows:

---

* James Henderson (1809-96) was educated at Marischal College, Aberdeen, until his father's death in 1826. Thereafter he studied architecture at evening classes in the Mechanics Institute. He was briefly in partnership with his brother William who, like James, was responsible for many Free Churches and manses in the Northeast. New Marnoch was James Henderson's first church; Forgue Free Church at Auchaber (1843) and possibly Drumblade (1843) are other local examples.[27]
(A comparison of the OS maps on page 29 shows that the original plans did not include the present Session Room adjoining Main Street. This was in fact added in 1875, again to a design by James Henderson, who in a letter to the Deacons Court stated his great satisfaction in presenting the plans as he had also had in presenting those of the church in 1841.[28] This later addition accounts for the curious positioning of the church windows relative to the Session Room.

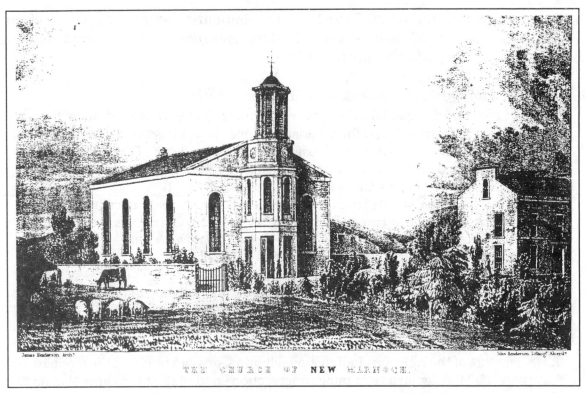

JAMES HENDERSON'S SKETCH OF THE CHURCH AND MANSE OF NEW MARNOCH

CHURCH	
Mason - James Barron, Macduff	£ 390 0s 0d
Carpenter/Slater/Plaster/Plumber -	
James Simpson, Aberdeen	£ 783 0s 0d
TOTAL (CHURCH)	£1173 0s 0d
MANSE	
Mason - Scott & Morrison, Macduff	£ 195 0s 0d
Carpenter - Strachan & McBeth, Fordyce	£ 207 10s 0d
Slater - John McCulloch, Banff	£ 21 14s 0d
Plaster - Ferguson & Lyon, Portsoy	£ 37 10s 6d
TOTAL (MANSE)	£ 461 14s 6d
TOTAL (CHURCH AND MANSE)	£1634 14s 6d *

---

*   The final cost of the new church and manse was quoted in the *Huntly Express* in 1864 as £3000 [29] and the *Banffshire Journal* in 1870 as £1800. [30] However, the audited accounts of the Heads of Families minute book provide these figures:

Amount collected		**£3030 8s 6 1/2d**
Expenses:	Ground and charter	£ 135 0s 0d
	Church	£1242 6s 6d
	Manse	£ 550 13s 6 1/2d
	Other expenses (roads, dykes, sheds, adverts, etc)	£ 277 3s 0 1/2d
Total expenses		**£2330 7s 1d**

- leaving approximately £700 in the bank in Edinburgh. [31] (See page 26.)

Just over ten weeks later, on 29 June 1841, the foundation stone for the new church was laid in the presence of the trustees and elders, congregation and many people from other parishes - about 2000 people in all.*

The Heads of Families minute book describes the occasion:
> After the congregation had joined in praise and prayer had been offered up by the Rev D Henry, Mr Stronach laid the foundation stone and addressed the assembly, after which the whole retired to the Causewayend quarry - where Divine worship was performed and an excellent sermon preached by Rev H Gordon - Minister of Montquhitter - from I Peter 4 Chap 12 - v. [i.e. I Peter Ch4,v.12]
> A bottle was deposited by Mr Stronach in the foundation stone - immediately under the South East angle of the Tower - containing the different Curt. coins - copies of the *Aberdeen Banner - Edinburgh witness - Glasgow Scottish Guardian & Dundee Warder* newspapers** ...and the following inscription on parchment -
> "New Marnoch - 29th June 1841 -
> This church is erected for the Glory of God & the accommodation of the parishioners of Marnoch by funds*** contributed by their Christian Brethern in Scotland - England - Ireland & America - who sympathise with them in being driven from their Parish Church -
> It is a measure of the righteous indignation felt by a Christian public at the forcible intrusion of a Minister on a reclaiming congregation - and of their high approbation of the present struggle of the Church of Scotland**** in defence of her spiritual independence, & the Christian rights & liberties of her people.
> The foundation stone is laid by Wm Stronach Esq - Ardmeallie - on this 29th day of June 1841 -
> The first Minr. is Revd. D Henry - The elders are - Messrs John Murray - Mains of Pittendreich - George Andrew - Euchrie - Alexr. Innes - Mill of Kinnairdy - James Robertson & William Allan - Aberchirder - all of whom along with Mr Stronach & Messrs Wm Grant Mill of Auchintoul - Wm. Wilson - Littlefield - James Wilson - Mains of Cranna - James Stephen, Dundee - & Alexr. Lyon - Culvie - constitute the Committee of Management..." [32]

The *Aberdeen Journal* [33] mentions that after the religious services, a large party of parishioners and several guests sat down to dinner in a tent near Mrs Allan's Inn.

The minute book goes on:
> During the summer of 1841 the work of building both church & manse was proceeded with. The committee held several meetings & arranged with Workmen for the building of the Dykes - Levelling - trenching & draining of the ground. During the year the Congregation worshipped in detachments at a shed by the riverside at the Inch Line & in the large building in the back street of the village of Aberchirder.***** [34]

---

*   These included Mr Troup of the *Aberdeen Banner*. [35]

**   All well known for their nonintrusionist sympathies.

***   See page 14.

****   See page 20.

*****   See footnote * on page 19.

OPENING OF THE CHURCH

The minute book recounts that the opening ceremony took place on 17 March 1842, with a sermon from Psalm 127 v.1 preached by Mr Elder of St Paul's Church, Edinburgh.** The bell was presented by John Duncan, the advocate who had helped the congregation throughout their dispute.

NEW MARNOCH CHURCH

---

*   The sawpit referred to on page 10, and the empty factory referred to on page 12, also in this letter to Mr Henry from Dr Candlish:

Edinburgh 17 Feb 1841

My Dear Sir,
I find I must proceed northwards next week to open the new church at Huntly on Friday the 26th. Can I be of any use to you on the Sabbath following, the 28th? - I must remain over that day, & I am willing to preach to the Marnoch folks, if you wish it, in the sawpit, or factory, or both, provided you dont ask more than two diets.

Yours very truly
Robt Candlish   36

(This was the first time the Inchline station was used for worship.) 37

**   Mr Henry had hoped to have an important figure to open the church, and the previous Moderator, Dr Makellar, had been approached without success. Eventually Robert Elder agreed to come, but only if the church was ready by 16 March, as Mrs Elder expected to give birth before the end of the month! 38

A document in the possession of Clifford Sandison, written in 1896 by Maggie Auchinachie, relates that the first person baptised in New Marnoch was Barbara Auchinachie* on 17 April 1842.

The settlement of the Rev David Henry took place on 22 July 1842, in the presence of a crowded congregation:

> ...As the settlement was in violation of an interdict by the Court of Session, the Presbytery of Strathbogie** was on the occasion assisted...by the Revd. C J Brown, Edin - The Revd. A D Davidson Aberdn - Revd. Mr Simpson Aberdn & Dr Smytton Elder Edin - who had been appointed by the General Assembly*** for this purpose - The Revd. Mr Dewar, Bellie, being Moderator of Pby officiated & preached from Colossians I Chapt 28 v. [39]

New Marnoch thus became

> the first Free Church in Scotland. We are aware that the south claims the honour for Auchterarder, but it rests with Marnoch. Auchterarder was in court first, but...must yield to Marnoch the distinction of being the first Free Church in Scotland. [40]

As the minute book mentions in a footnote added later, there was a price to pay for independence:

> The Presbytery & the above mentioned individuals & Mr Henry were afterwards summoned to the bar of the Court of Session & fined 5£ (sic) each for breach of Interdict! [41]

THE DISRUPTION

While New Marnoch Church was being built in Aberchirder, the Evangelicals at national level, led by Dr Thomas Chalmers, issued a Claim Of Right in May 1842. This argued that the state had a duty to maintain the Church of Scotland, but had no right to interfere with the government of the Church. To this the civil courts responded in August 1842 in a statement by Lord Campbell, who said that the Established Church, because it was subsidised by the state, must obey the civil law. Sir Robert Peel, the Prime Minister, also stated that the Church must be subordinate to the state.

---

*   Barbara was a member of the family which was to provide two provosts of Aberchirder - William Auchinachie, first provost 1893-1907, who presented the fountain in the Square to mark the diamond jubilee of Queen Victoria in 1897, and another William, provost 1932-1947. Both ran a draper's and general merchant's shop at 11 The Square (now the New Image hairdressing salon). The elder William had joined the Free Church but later left to join the Church of Christ, which met above his shop. This Church eventually faded away in the 1930s as its predominantly elderly members died off. [42]

**   These were the members who had not been suspended by the General Assembly, including the Rev David Brown of Ord (see page 34).

*** At this time the Assembly was controlled by the Evangelicals.

Brown [43] summed up the Evangelicals' view of the problem:
> Had the Church of Scotland, because Established, lost the right to be guided by her own conscientious convictions on a matter so obviously spiritual as the forming of a pastoral tie?

The Evangelicals were further disturbed by the final decision on the Auchterarder case, when in 1842 the House of Lords awarded £10 000 damages against the presbytery in favour of the patron's nominee - which meant that all presbyteries which tried to implement the Veto Act were now liable to be sued.

The final straw came when the Moderates in the Church of Scotland officially resolved to support the Strathbogie ministers whom the Assembly had suspended. This led the Evangelicals to see the Moderates as
> a combination within the Church itself for the overthrow of that sacred authority which she held from Christ, her head. [44]

In November 1842, a Convocation of 474 nonintrusion ministers from all over Scotland was held in Edinburgh. Inspired by Dr Chalmers, they resolved to stand by their belief in spiritual independence and, if necessary, to leave the Established Church.

DR THOMAS CHALMERS

Over the winter of 1842-1843 the Convocation ministers used public meetings to put their case to congregations throughout Scotland - whether the local minister agreed or not! - and there was great public interest.

In early 1843 both Government and the House of Commons rejected the Evangelicals' views, and by March Dr Chalmers was ready for a split. Two months later, on 17 May, on the eve of the General Assembly, the Evangelicals held a conference at which 400 ministers signed the protest which Dr Welsh, the retiring Moderator, was to lay on the table of the Assembly, renouncing the Establishment. And a hall to hold 300 had been prepared at Tanfield, near Canonmills.

Next afternoon, led by Dr Welsh, nearly 200 ministers and elders walked out of the Assembly, watched by large crowds in the streets outside. At Tanfield Hall, Dr Chalmers was elected Moderator of the Free Assembly, which from 18 to 30 May worked on producing the Deed of Demission, by which its members gave up their churches and manses in the Established Church. This document was then signed at a public meeting by 474 Free Church ministers, who thereby gave up more than £100 000 a year in incomes. [45] (It should also be noted that in some cases where the minister of a church did not secede, the bulk of the congregation left.) [46]

THE FIRST FREE CHURCH ASSEMBLY - SIGNING THE DEED OF DEMISSION

The ministers who had seceded now faced a hard time, with no church, no manse and no income. In many cases the landowner's opposition made it very difficult to find even temporary accommodation for worship.

THE FREE CHURCH

The new Church quickly set about a rapid building programme, financed by a general building fund to which wealthy town congregations and poor country ones contributed as much as they could afford, and received equal shares back. By May 1847, after only four years, over 700 churches had been built.

A similar scheme for building manses raised £116 370 by May 1846, which allowed £150-£200 to be put towards each manse, the rest coming from local subscriptions. [47]

Ministers were paid out of a Sustentation Fund devised by Dr Chalmers. In each parish, collectors went round families at least once a month, and the money raised was sent to a central fund in Edinburgh. From this ministers got an equal payment, to which each congregation had to add as much as it could afford. [48] This led in some cases to big drops in income; for example, Dr McFarlan at Greenock - reckoned to be the best living in Scotland - had been on £780 a year and now got £317 (without a house), while one country minister in Ayrshire dropped from £350 to about £120 (without a house). [49]

One final programme to be undertaken was the building of Free Church schools. Just as the Established Church had, since the Reformation, seen provision of church schools as a priority, in order to educate children in the 'true religion', so the Free Church now wanted to ensure that its members' children were brought up to worship according to its beliefs. Within a year £52 000 had been collected, and a year after that there were already 280 schools in operation. Many of the teachers in the new schools were ones who had been left without a job because of the Disruption. [50]

NEW MARNOCH JOINS THE FREE CHURCH

Once the Free Church had been set up, New Marnoch Church was quick to join. The first entry in the minute book of the Free Church Kirk Session, for 15 June 1843, reads:

> Which day the Kirk Session being met & constituted with prayer - Sedt. Revd. David Henry Moderator* - Messrs John Murray - George Andrew - Willm. Allan - James Robertson - & Alexr. Innes Elders - The Kirk Session - taking into consideration the circumstances in which they are now placed - by the disruption of the Church of Scotland - whereby nearly five Hundred Ministers have seceded from the Establishment...constitute themselves a Kirk Session in Connection with Said Church & signed the...Act of Demission by the Elders of the Free Church of Scotland - approved by the General Assembly at Edinburgh 26 May 1843 - (The Moderator having previously signed the Deed of Demission by Ministers...) [51]

The Deacons Court of New Marnoch was elected by the congregation on 26 December 1843 and installed on 2 January 1844.**

---

*   (of the Kirk Session)

**   The members of the Deacons Court were: Wm. Mitchell, Culvie; James Taylor, Tillydown; Wm. Reid, Crombie; James Redford, Corskie; Alex. Skene, Elrick; John Cooper, Knockorth; Alex. Brebner, Janefield; Peter Reid, Janefield; Wm. Milne, Aberchirder; Wm. Stronach, Ardmeallie; Charles Thomson, Cluny; Wm. Walker, Harperhill; Geo. Imlach, Gladfield. [52]

Records show that even after New Marnoch had been built, services continued to be held in other premises:

> [After New Marnoch was built] occasional services...were held in barns round about, or at "The Inchline", where a wooden building was erected for the convenience of those in the south-west of the parish, and where Mr Henry usually preached once-a-fortnight on the Sabbath evenings. [53]

The Deacons Court minutes include annual accounts which show collections from the Inchline station amounting to about £3 a year until 1858, and rent paid for the Inchline station is listed till 1867; Crombie station is mentioned in the years 1867-70, with annual collections of between 11s to 16s. [54] (These figures compare with collections in New Marnoch of between £300 and £500 a year.)

And in 1871

> ...agreed that the local Elders and Deacons take charge of the collections made at the various stations where diets of public worship are held on the Sabbath evenings and hand them in half-yearly. [55]

GAS LIGHTING IN NEW MARNOCH

One of the first improvements to the new church was the installation of gas lighting:

> Church fitted with gas lighting - work to be done by Mr Lewis Paul, Rothiemay - £80 spent 1844 on building gashouse & fitting equipment. [56]

> 13 Nov 1844
> The church was for the first time, this evening lighted with gas. [57]

The gas was acetylene, and the accounts show regular entries for purchase of the lime and coal used in making it.

The *Huntly Express* noted in 1864 that

> at nights the church is lighted up with gas (not yet extended to the village) which streams in living jets from seventy burners. [58]

(By late 1936 the Grampian Electric Supply Company was bringing electricity to Aberchirder. After a special fund-raising effort electric light was installed in New Marnoch church and manse in 1938-39. It was not until 1961-62 that electric lighting and heating were installed at Marnoch Church.)

THE CHURCH AND MORALS

One of the Church of Scotland's vital roles in society had always been the supervision of the morals of parishioners, and the cutty stool had been the fate of many a sinner. Although the stool of repentance was no longer in use by the 1840s, the minutes of the Kirk Sessions of both Marnoch and New Marnoch soon turn from the excitements of the Marnoch Case to the routine business of dealing with fornicators.

A typical entry reads:

2 July 1843

...Appeared James A and Jane T - voluntarily confessing themselves guilty of the sin of fornication - being suitably admonished regarding the nature of the sin - having several passages of scripture pointed out to them for their serious consideration - they were laid under Church censure & ordered to appear again. [59]

Many cases, however, concerned antenuptial fornication, which involved recently married couples who had been a trifle impatient. In fact, in the 1840s this offence accounted for about 30% of all cases. Some sinners appear in the records more than once, admitting to relapse (second offence), trilapse (third offence) or even quadrilapse (fourth offence). James P of Craignetherty actually appeared twice in 1848 admitting to fornication with two different parishioners!

The big scandal of the 1840s showed that, despite the ecclesiastical rupture at Marnoch, at least some of the members of the rival congregations were obviously still on good terms. In 1847 William B, an elder of Marnoch, confessed to being the father of the illegitimate child of Helen C, a member of New Marnoch (whose own Kirk Session duly disciplined her). Marnoch Kirk Session,

having considered the great scandal which he has given to the Christian community to which he belonged [60]

remitted the case to the Presbytery, which duly issued a sentence which was read out from the pulpit, namely to

depose said William B from his office as an Elder of this Church, and prohibit him from exercising any of the functions thereof in all time coming... [61]

Two months later he was, however, deemed penitent enough to be restored to ordinary membership. Alas, four years later Helen C again appeared before Marnoch Kirk Session,

confessing herself guilty of a relapse in fornication and charging William B... as her partner in guilt [62]...The said William B being called compeared, and acknowledged his guilt...and having been suitably admonished was dismissed in the meantime. [63]

Three months later the Kirk Session again accepted William B's profession of repentance, and released him from further discipline. [64]

A touching case in 1889 concerned [Miss] NW, who confessed to fornication with a nonresident of the village.

Her position as a young communicant and her present standing were solemnly compared, and her attention drawn to the lesson accruing therefrom. [65]

This role of the Church continued well into the 20th Century, although decreasing steadily - the last entry for Old Marnoch is for 1934 and for New Marnoch 1946.

The minutes of the Deacons Court show that, as for the Free Church nationally*, education was one of the top priorities of New Marnoch, and a Free Church school with male and female departments was set up in 1844. The minute book of the Heads of Families mentions that this was possible because there was still £700 in the bank at the beginning of that year.**

After several public meetings, property in North Street was bought from Mr Aitken of Auchintoul for £110, and a charter on it obtained, dated 6 May 1844. [66] These were the
> extensive premises...that Mr Morison of Auchintoul had erected and intended for a factory***...and part of it was fitted up as a first classroom...
> There is no doubt that this school started well and was very successful. Mr Robert Nicol was in charge of the male school, and taught there for 32 years; Miss Reach was the teacher of the girls' department. [67]

The school was financed by fees charged as follows:

MALE DEPARTMENT

English Reading			2s	per qr
Do	& Writing		2s6d	..
Do	Do	+ Arithmetic	3s	..
Grammar (English)			6d	..
Geography			6d	..
Latin			5s	..
Mensuration, Mathematics, &c			5s	..

FEMALE DEPARTMENT

Reading & Sewing	2s6d	.. [68]

Two other Free Church schools were built in the parish, at Culvie and Blacklaw. The one at Culvie was erected during the summer of 1844 on ground leased for a rent of 5s a year [69] by Robert Ogilvie of Culvie, to answer the needs of the inhabitants of the northwest part of the parish. Mr John Urquhart taught at this school, which stood where the farm of Ryefield now stands. [70] The school at Blacklaw was built**** largely thanks to the efforts of the Rev Henry, who on Marnan Fair day 1862 organised a very successful bazaar in Aberchirder which raised £90 towards the project. [71]

---

*   See page 23.

**   See footnote * on page 17.

***   See pages 12 and 19.

****   Barclay quotes the opening date as 1862, but the building shows the date 1866.

The annual salaries paid to the teachers were:

Mr Nicol (incl. fees as clerk of the Deacons Court)	£6 10s
Miss Reach	£2 *
Mr Urquhart	£1 [72]

In Aberchirder, the school premises were not large enough for the numbers of pupils - usually about 200 - attending, and in April 1855 an appeal was issued to the congregation:

> ...The Managers have resolved upon the erection of a new [school]...They find that notwithstanding the means available a subscription is necessary, and the Managers would appeal to the generosity of the congregation and other friends in order that they may be enabled to erect a healthful and more commodious building. [73]

This appeal to the congregation realised £151 14s 5d and, together with existing funds, allowed the church to build a new school in North Street. Ex-Provost Gregor of Cullen**, who had attended the Church of Scotland school (see page 28) recalled:

> There was at that time what was termed the Free Kirkers' School, where the present town hall is in North Street...Many a battle was fought between us in the winter time with snowballs. There was another school beside the Free Kirk school in the house facing the street ***...[74]

These schools can be seen on the 1866 OS map of Aberchirder, on page 29.

THE 1850s FREE CHURCH SCHOOL - NOW THE SUPPER ROOM OF THE MEMORIAL HALL

---

*   £3 in years when it could be afforded!

**   Father of John Gregor, longtime New Marnoch Session Clerk and local headmaster, and Provost of Aberchirder 1947-49.

***   This was a separate, privately run girls' school (see 1866 map on page 29).

Marnoch parish school had always been near Marnoch Church, and by the 19th Century a Church of Scotland school also provided education in the village. After the Disruption the Established Church continued to operate a school there, in various locations:

> It was for a time in buildings next the Fife Arms Hotel - "Annie Gray's Inn" was its popular name in those days; it was also, with an entrance by an outside stair from the back, in the upper apartments of what is now the Temperance Hotel on the Square *; and when it was removed in 1862 to the lower end of the burgh **, it became the nucleus of the...Public and Secondary School of Aberchirder. [75]

This - what is now the Old School, used by Bremner's of Foggie - was the result of the School Board, set up in 1873, combining all the existing village schools. Two new classrooms were added to the Church of Scotland school, at a cost of £1000, of which Mr Stronach of Ardmeallie contributed £100. [76] (These buildings were virtually rebuilt in 1901, and later underwent further alterations.)

As a result of the combining of schools in 1873, the Free Church school in North Street became the Town Hall, which is now the supper room at the rear of the Memorial Hall. This new hall, which was added to the original one to commemorate those who lost their lives in the First World War, was started in 1925 and officially opened in October 1926, with a joint religious service led by the Established and Free Church ministers. [77]

THE OLD SCHOOL - NOW BREMNER'S OF FOGGIE

---

*   (Now a private house, No.12 The Square, at the southwest junction of Main Street and The Square.)

**   See 1866 map on page 29.

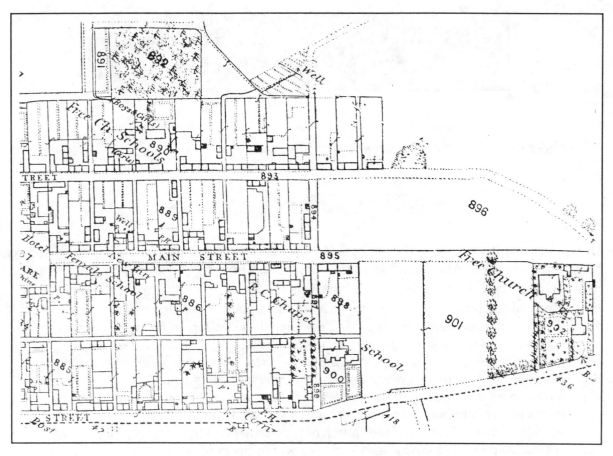

OS MAP OF ABERCHIRDER : 1ST EDITION 1866

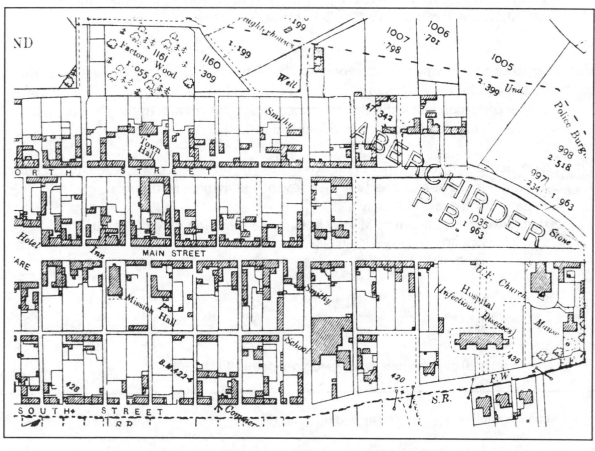

OS MAP OF ABERCHIRDER : 2ND EDITION 1904

What became of the main figures in the Marnoch case?

THE REV JOHN EDWARDS

In the aftermath of the walkout in 1841, Mr Edwards was left with a much reduced congregation. The *Aberdeen Journal*, possibly allowing editorial bias to creep in, reported the situation in the Old Church as follows:

> Many of our readers will be happy to learn that appearances already indicate a different state of feeling in the parish, from what the leaders of the opposition to Mr Edwards and the Non-Intrusion prints would have led the public to believe...On the last Lord's Day [31 January] he [Mr Edwards] preached a very excellent sermon, from 1st Tim i,16, to an increased congregation, numbering from 110 to 120; among whom, notwithstanding all the lively imaginings and graphic descriptions of the editor of a certain Non-Intrusion contemporary* regarding the fast-flowing tears of the aged when driven from the church of their fathers on the 21st ult., - there were several respectable-looking aged and grey worshippers of both sexes. Mr Edwards' discourse, we are informed, was listened to with devout attention by the congregation who, by their whole demeanour, gave evidence of a feeling of kindly welcome to their pastor. The offering, amounting to upwards of eighteen shillings, was collected by James and Patrick Rose Innes, Esquires, of Netherdale.** [78]

However, this rather optimistic report of the extent of support for Mr Edwards was contradicted by the next item of news from Marnoch in the same paper, stating:

> Another correspondent states that the congregation did not amount to 100; and that they were composed of persons from [other parishes] besides Marnoch. [79]

This latter account agrees with evidence from a letter sent to the Rev Henry, which suggests that Mr Edwards was left with few of his own parishioners:

> [No date, but approx. 15 March 1841]
>
> **Attendance at the Church of Marnoch Since the Intrusion of Mr Edwards**

		Dismissed after the Blessing	
January	31		59
February	7		70
	14		67
	21		85
	28		32
March	7		38
	14		80

[Then names 20 parishioners who were present on 14 March.]

---

*   Almost certainly a dig at Mr Troup and the *Banner*!

**   See footnote * on page 36.

...The other members of the congregation were collected from the Parishes of Fivie Turriff Auchterless Inverkeithnie Forgue Rothiemay Grange Keith Ordiquhill Boyndie & Forglen.

Alexander Bremner [80]

But despite these figures in the aftermath of the breakaway, it is claimed that
by his prudent and conciliatory manners he won much esteem and affection from many of his parishioners and from those who had been his opponents. [81]

However Mr Edwards, after his long legal battle to be installed as minister of Old Marnoch, lived until only 1848. As the Kirk Session minutes recorded:
The Reverend John Edwards minister of this parish died at two oclock on the morning of Sunday the 1st October, and was buried on Friday October 6th 1848. [82]

Mr Edwards had been taken ill about five weeks before his death
with general debility, arising from weakness of the lungs. At one time he was thought to have nearly recovered, but on the Thursday before his death, he again became seriously ill; the disease assumed the form of congestion of the brain, and...it proceeded with increasing virulence...The reverend gentleman was, on Friday morning, apprised by Dr Whyte of Banff, of the serious nature of the disorder, and its probable fatal issue. He received the intelligence with the utmost composure, and immediately prepared himself...He has left a widow, but no family. [83]

Mr Edwards' gravestone is in the parish graveyard, near the river.

**GRAVESTONES OF THE REV JOHN EDWARDS AND THE REV DAVID HENRY
IN OLD MARNOCH CHURCHYARD**

The *Banffshire Journal* obituary also supported the view that Mr Edwards had won some popularity since his intrusion:

> Never was any minister more deeply and sincerely regretted by a parish. During his illness, the enquiries regarding him were numerous and affectionate...When his death became known at...Aberchirder, there was but one feeling of the profoundest grief, and...an old woman...said "Aye, he's awa'. Weel, it will mak muckle difference in this parish, for he was aye kind to them that didna like him."...At his last [communion]...the number of communicants present were within two or three of 200. We may also mention, as a proof of his great popularity, that during the last twelve months, he has, at the request of the villagers, preached every second Sabbath evening in the village of Marnoch...The place of meeting was a large hall*, capable of holding about 300 people, and such were the numbers that flocked to hear him, that it was very seldom that all who came were able to find accommodation. [84]

Under Mr Edwards' successors, the numbers on the communicants' roll at Old Marnoch rose from 41 in 1842 to 453 in 1868 and 622 in 1900, despite a falling population. [85] This progress was commented on by the Old Marnoch Kirk Session in their tribute to the Rev Alexander Anderson following his death in 1880:

> ...The Church of Marnoch has prospered greatly...the number of communicants having risen from about 180 at his induction [in 1848] to about 462 at his death. [86]

The same minute also notes that

> his efforts in providing a mission station* at Aberchirder are specially deserving of record and had his life been spared the Kirk Session cannot doubt that he would have erelong succeeded in the erection and endowment of a church there, an object near to his heart, and for which he had already begun to labour. [87]

In fact an Established church was later built in Aberchirder - though it has usually been referred to as the Church Hall - see page 38.

THE REV DAVID HENRY

Mr Henry served as minister of New Marnoch till his death in 1870, aged 65. The obituary in the *Banffshire Journal* stated:

> Mr Henry was held in very high esteem. Certainly it is given to very few clergymen to maintain for such a lengthened period as he did so high a standard of pulpit ministrations, and at the same time work so laboriously in his district...In the parish he wrought incessantly, travelling much on foot, and visiting the sick with unusual frequency...A noticeable characteristic of Mr Henry was his studious care for the well-being of the aged... [88]

And Mr Henry's sermons had been praised by the author of an article on Marnoch parish in the *Huntly Express* in 1864:

> The sermon occupied exactly three-quarters of an hour, and the attention of the audience was very close - so close, indeed, that we saw only two persons asleep during the service. [89] (!)

---

*   Unfortunately there is no record of which premises these refer to - possibly the Temperance Hotel (see page 28)?

THE REV DAVID HENRY

Mr Henry died at 3 am on 7 October 1870, He had been in indifferent health for several years, and had preached his last sermon on 15 May of that year. A short stay at Strathpeffer spa had

> failed to remove, or even mitigate, the disease preying on his vitals, and after his return to Marnoch all hopes of recovery had to be abandoned. He was afflicted with paralysis in the lower extremities of his body...
>
> The body was removed to the church on Tuesday...
>
> The funeral, which was a public one, took place on Thursday; and notwithstanding the uncomfortable weather, was attended by 500 persons, about 360 of whom walked in procession, four abreast, the others being conveyed in machines. Upwards of twenty ministers of...various denominations were present. The services in the church were conducted by Mr Dewar of Fochabers and Mr Moffat of Cairnie. [90]

In their tribute to Mr Henry, the Kirk Session recorded:

> He rebuked, exhorted, warned, visited with much zeal, patience and affection...and left...in sinner saved and saints edified, evidences not a few of the success of his ministry. [91]

At a congregational meeting on 5 July 1871

> Mr Stronach proposed that a Memorial Tablet to the late revered Minister be erected in the church. The meeting...agreed...and collectors were named in the various districts to collect the necessary funds. [92]

It is somewhat ironic that Mr Henry was buried in Marnoch Churchyard, no more than 20 yards from his rival, Mr Edwards!

MR WILLIAM STRONACH

Mr Stronach remained active as an elder and deacon until 1877, and lived long enough to attend the 50th anniversary celebrations of New Marnoch Church in 1891, at the age of 96.

MR WILLIAM STRONACH

On Sunday 20 June 1891, a series of four services was held in the church - two taken by Principal Rainy of New College, Edinburgh, one by Mr Paterson, Glasgow (father of the then assistant minister at New Marnoch) and one by another survivor of the secession, Principal David Brown (minister of Ord at the time of the Disruption).

The Monday programme, attended by large crowds who had taken time off work for the celebrations, consisted of a conference of ministers and office-bearers at 11:30 am; a public banquet for about 150 in the Public Hall, catered by Mrs Steel, New Inn, at 2:30 pm; and a social meeting in the church at 6:30 pm. The conference was officially to discuss the privileges and responsibilities of office-bearers, but most speeches were in celebration of the Disruption and Marnoch's part in it!

The highlight of the conference for the *Huntly Express* reporter came when Mr Stronach was led in

> with cheeks pale and sunken, hair white as the driven snow, hands and limbs shaky and uncertain, and yet with eyes bright, piercing and intelligent as of yore. This is the man - the connecting link between the present and the past - whose entrance brought the hearts of men and women to their throats...It was a marvellous coincidence that the man who had played so important a part in the first days of battle should have been spared to countenance...the jubilee of the congregation and of the Church... And now close beside him stood Principal Brown, who had been at his side on the

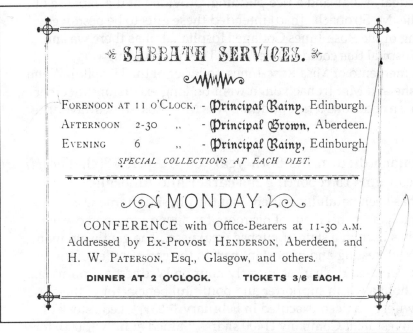

PROGRAMME FOR THE 1891 JUBILEE CELEBRATION AT MARNOCH FREE CHURCH

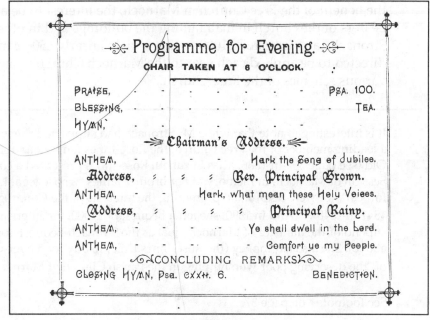

eventful day [of the walkout]...It took Mr Stronach but a moment to recognise his old friend. How can words depict the touching scene which followed!...There stood the two veterans of the fight, and in the presence of all the people they fondly embraced and kissed each other. No wonder that tears trickled down both their faces, or that their voices trembled with violent emotion...meeting in every likelihood for the last time until they both reach the presence of the Church's King and Lord...After sitting about two hours - taking a lively interest in what was going on - Mr Stronach signified that he wished to go home...Then with one arm linked in each of the Principals the old man stood up and facing the people - his eyes full of tears and yet his face radiant with smiles - he said, "Forever goodbye - God bless you!"
It was a solemn moment. All was hushed, and it seemed, indeed, as if God was present in the midst of His people. Men and women sobbed aloud, tears flowed freely, and as the form of the grand old man disappeared from the church all could not but feel that his journey on earth must soon be over. [93]

In fact Mr Stronach lived a further two years, and continued to take an interest in those less fortunate than himself:

On Hogmanay night, each of 80 registered poor residing in Aberchirder received the gift of 4oz of tea, 2lb of sugar, 1 loaf, and a rice pudding, provided at the expense of Mr Stronach of Ardmellie. Mr Stronach...[had] intended these gifts to be bestowed on the day of the opening of the Rose-Innes Cottage Hospital...but as there was no formal opening of the Hospital this could not be done. The rice pudding was intended especially as a memento of Miss Rose-Innes, founder of the Hospital. When both were very young, she and Mr Stronach often went on long excursions together on horseback, and on those occasions a rice pudding was Miss Rose-Innes' favourite repast. [94] *

Finally, however, Mr Stronach died in his 98th year, on 5 April 1893. The *Huntly Express* devoted over two columns to reporting his career and funeral:

...For some time past it has been painfully evident that the physical frame was breaking up. Mr Stronach had not been out of his room for a long time, and during the last week or two he has been in a state of intense weakness...The gentle old man, who had played such an interesting and important part in the early battles of the Free Church of Scotland, "crossed the bar" at an early hour on Wednesday morning... Mr Stronach was throughout a warm supporter and bountiful benefactor of the church; and he and his wife, by a deed executed in February 1883, placed...stock of the Scottish Australian Investment Company (1400 shares, valued at fully £3000) for the benefit of the Free Church in Marnoch, the interest to be applied by the office-bearers of the church in maintaining the buildings and in other ways**...Mr and Mrs Stronach...also invested £1000 so that it yields nearly £50 yearly. This sum was directed to be applied each year to the Marnoch Church's contributions to the various schemes of the Free Church...

---

*   It is interesting to note that while Mr Stronach had supported the walkout in 1841, and had become a leading member of the Free Church, the Rose-Innes family had remained members of Marnoch Old (see page 30). In 1886, Miss Elizabeth Rose-Innes presented a communion service to the Kirk Session of Marnoch, in memory of her brother James "whose legal knowledge and kind Christian forbearance were helpful...in promoting the interests of the Congregation during the period from 1841 to 1848". [95] And in 1890, she left a bequest of £1000, the interest to be used to supplement the stipend of the minister of Marnoch - just as the Stronach Bequest applied to New Marnoch (see above). She also left money (the Rose-Innes Dole) to buy food every Christmas Day for the relief of "the deserving poor worshipping in the Parish Church of Marnoch". [96]

**   See footnote * on page 37.

THE FUNERAL

took place yesterday [Friday 7 April 1893] from Ardmellie to the churchyard of Rothiemay. All the arrangements for the interment were of the simplest character, special instructions...having been left by the deceased...The mould with which the coffin was covered when committed to the earth was taken from a favourite nook within the grounds at Ardmellie. Previous to the removal of the body, an impressive service was conducted in the house by Rev Mr Johnstone, Free Church minister in Marnoch, assisted by Rev Mr Allan, minister of the parish, and the Rev Mr M'Raith, United Presbyterian Church, Aberchirder...**

By twelve o'clock, for which hour the funeral had been fixed, a large concourse of people from the surrounding districts had paid their last respects...A number of those present followed on foot for a considerable distance, in addition to a procession of some twenty carriages and other vehicles...On entering the churchyard the whole company uncovered their heads and remained there until the coffin had been placed in its last resting place - beside the remains of the late Mrs Stronach. The Stronach family have been interred in this plot of ground for many generations back.*** A little granite slab at the top of the vault in which the remains were yesterday placed bears the following interesting and as yet unfinished epitaph:

188
-

WM STRONACH, RL. ENGRS
3RD SON OF REV. WM STRONACH
DIED
IN HIS   YEAR
AND
ANNA ORROCK, HIS WIFE
DIED 3RD DEC. 1888
IN HER 87TH YEAR
AFTER A WEDDED LIFE OF
67 YEARS AT ARDMEALLIE
AND REST HERE TOGETHER
IN FAITH
-

NOT TO BE OPENED FOR ANY
FUTURE PURPOSE****

There was no service at the graveside, and the only sounds that broke the solemn stillness were the songs of the birds and the murmuring of the river*****...And with such a requiem was left all that was mortal of the man whose name will be spoken of and remembered so long as man delight to tell of decisive blows struck for political and ecclesiastical liberty, of lives honourably and fearlessly lived in the desire to do good and to leave the world better than they found it...[97]

---

*   These included a sum of £40 a year to be added to the minister's stipend, and £30 a year to any minister forced to retire due to ill-health. [98]

**   This may be taken as a sign that by then any old animosities had gone.

***   Inscriptions on the main slab run from James Stronach, 2nd son of Alexander Stronach of Knock, died 29 August 1777, aged 20 years, to the Rev William Stronach, died 11 April 1837.

**** The completed inscription is now rather blurred, and the top date could read either '1888' or '1893'; '5TH APRIL' was added after 'DIED'; and '98TH' between 'HIS' and 'YEAR'.

***** In fact the sound would have been that of the burn that flows past the back wall of the graveyard on its way to the River Deveron.

THE CHURCH HALL

Old Marnoch Church had held services in Aberchirder for many years* before it was decided to build a Church Hall in the village:

> The Kirk Session taking into consideration the inconvenience of the Public School in Aberchirder for the Evening Services resolved to take steps for the Erection of a suitable Church Hall to hold at least 300... [99]

Properties at 80-84 Main Street were bought from Robert Sim, at a price of £108. Plans were obtained from Messrs Duncan & Son, Turriff [100] and Alexander McHardy's estimate of £707 17s for all building costs was accepted. [101] Funds were raised from the Church of Scotland Home Mission Committee (7s6d per sitting of 20 inches - £138 in all) [102], the Baird Trust (£200) [103] and £612 2s raised locally by subscription - much of it in very small sums collected by the Rev Allan and the elders on congregational visits. The total raised, £950 2s, was enough to pay for the hall outright.**

The building of the Hall, which was formally opened on 19 March 1899, was timely in that it could be used as temporary accommodation by the Public School while its major alterations were taking place in 1901. [104] ***

In the succeeding years the Hall provided facilities for many of the social and cultural activities of the village, including meetings of guides, scouts, Red Cross and Masonic Lodge****, as well as performances by Aberchirder Operatic Society, Choral Union and amateur dramatic groups.

During the Second World War the Hall was requisitioned by the Ministry of Food in 1942 for storing emergency food supplies [105] and only became available again for evening services in August 1945. [106]

From 1960 to 1967 the Church Hall was the venue for the newly formed Marnoch Church Indoor Bowling Club [107], which thereafter renamed itself the Aberchirder & District Indoor Bowling Club and in 1978 merged with the outdoor Aberchirder Bowling Club [108], not long before the highly successful expansion of that organisation through the 1980s.

In the television age, interest in musical and dramatic productions has declined, but the Church Hall still provides a valuable venue for the voluntary organisations and for the many fund-raising coffee mornings which form an important and popular part of village life. And on Sundays, it is the home of the Sunday School.

New Marnoch Church also had its church hall after 1907 - see page 40.

---

*   See page 32.

**   Marked on the 1904 map as the Mission Hall; the Kirk Session minutes refer to it as such until 1909, whereafter it is termed the Church Hall (or, by the Rev Edward Walker, as the Hall Church.)

***   See page 28.

****   Lodge Marnoch 1325 was formed in 1924. [109]

REUNION

In contrast to the disharmony of the 18th and 19th Centuries, the 20th Century has seen a steady process of reintegration among the Presbyterian Churches of Scotland, and this has been reflected in Marnoch.

The early 19th Century saw considerable acitvity by evangelical preachers in the area, and as early as 1792 the session of Grange Secession Church received a petition from some Marnoch residents asking for services to be held there. The Rev John Primrose, minister of Grange,

> preached there six Sabbaths about that time, when the roof was off the old parish church... [110]

In 1820 several secessionist groups at national level combined to form the United Secession Church. In 1826 it was reported that

> a preacher had lately conducted services at Foggieloan...where evangelical preaching was much needed. From this time a station was kept up, but it was not until 1839 that the people had sermon every Sabbath. [111]

This is corroborated by the recollections in 1889 (see below) of Mr Joseph Murray, an Aberchirder merchant and by then a member of the town's Baptist Church [112] :

> About 1823, the Seceders in Aberchirder petitioned the Synod for a supply of probationers to be sent...This was granted, the services being held in the Hall* in the after part of the day. Many able and devoted preachers came to Aberchirder, and much good was done. About 1838, some of the leading men in the church, Mr Bartlet, farmer, Carnousie...and others in Aberchirder became anxious to have a house of their own in which to worship and, as the result of their efforts, the present church was erected in the summer of 1839 and opened for divine service on Sunday, 17 November. [113]

Thus a United Secession Church with sittings for 350 was built in Aberchirder, at the junction of North Street and Cornhill Road. The cost was £270, of which the congregation raised £100 and the Mission Board granted £120. (The remaining debt was paid off by 1845 with the help of £30 from the Liquidation Fund.) By 1841 a congregation had been formed and elders elected. Membership was given as about 30 and attendance about 110, from a population of 800 in the village. [114]

In 1847 the United Secession Church merged with the Relief Church (another secessionist Church, formed in 1761) to form the United Presbyterian Church, with about 500 congregations throughout Scotland, and the North Street church became Aberchirder United Presbyterian Church. For most of the rest of the century the membership remained around the forty mark, but under the Rev John McRaith it rose to about 100. It was during his ministry that the church celebrated its jubilee on Friday 15 November 1889 with nothing more elaborate than a social meeting in the church, at which Mr Joseph Murray gave a speech recalling the history of dissenting congregations in Aberchirder (see above). [115] Soon afterwards the church was largely rebuilt at a cost of £350, being reopened on 9 June 1893. [116]

---

*　　The upper floor of the Temperance Hotel (see page 28).

The United Presbyterian and Free Churches differed on a number of issues, but by the end of the 19th Century a large majority of members of the Free Church were ready to unite with the UPs, and in 1900 the United Free Church of Scotland was formed. In Aberchirder the two churches concerned changed their names to New Marnoch United Free Church and West United Free Church of Aberchirder. They continued as two separate congregations until December 1906 when the retiral of the Rev John Ross from New Marnoch, and the willingness of the Rev McRaith of the West Church to retire, made a union possible, and Marnoch United Free Church came into being. The first united service took place on 13 January 1907 and the Rev Godfrey McFadyen was inducted in June of the following year. [117] The West Church became the West Hall (see below) and the West Manse (Hamewith, Cornhill Road) was eventually sold off for £625 in 1921. [118]

Meanwhile, in 1874 the Patronage Act had been repealed, and when Parliament declared the independence of the Established Church from the state in 1921 and 1925 the last obstacle to reunion between Free and Established Churches was removed.* So in October 1929 the United Free Church and Church of Scotland reunited, leaving Marnoch with two churches - Marnoch and New Marnoch - in use.

Wartime conditions meant that the centenary of New Marnoch passed quietly, with a special service on Sunday 29 June 1941, one hundred years to the day since the laying of the foundation stone.** The service, attended by a large congregation including people whose forebears were connected with the church in its early days, was conducted by Principal Adam Fyfe Findlay, Master of Christ's College Aberdeen, assisted by the Rev Percy Strachan, who was able to be home on leave from his duties as an army chaplain. [119] Principal Findlay paid tribute to the fight for spiritual independence in the Secession of 1733 and the Disruption of 1843, and especially by the men of Marnoch in 1841. [120]

THE WEST HALL

Before and after the reunion of 1929 the West Hall was, like its counterpart in Main Street, used by various youth and other groups - even at one stage as changing rooms for St Marnan's FC! [121] - and during the Second World War was used by the Home Guard.

After the war the Hall was bought in 1947 by Mr William Davidson of Cullen, a great-great-grandson of one of the original founders of the Aberchirder United Secession Church. [122] Mr Davidson ran the Hall as a cinema, showing three, and latterly two, programmes a week from 1950 till January 1959. The property was then sold to Mr A R Bremner, who donated the bell to New Church of Marnoch. [123] (The bell is currently stored on the roof of the Church Hall, as forlorn as the church where it was once rung.)

---

* During the 1920s the leading proponents of union in Marnoch were Charles Sandison on the Marnoch Kirk Session and Charles Geddes on the Marnoch UF Kirk Session. [124]

** See page 18.

Writing in 1951, the Rev Buchanan of Old Marnoch gave the impression that the religious fervour which had been expressed in the 1840s was no longer in evidence:

In Marnoch, there is little interest in theology or religious matters and to a great many the minister is merely an official who is there for the purpose of performing marriages and taking funeral services. Churchgoing is not the fashion and only 15 to 20 per cent of the congregation attend regularly. [However] the church has a warm place in the hearts of the people, who feel there is something lacking if their name is not on the roll. There is no hostility to religion and the minister receives a genuine welcome in every home. [125]

ORIGINAL
PROPOSALS FOR BASIS
OF UNION OF MARNOCH
AND NEW MARNOCH
CONGREGATIONS -
SUBSEQUENTLY
ALTERED

PRESBYTERY OF STRATHBOGIE.

BASIS OF UNION AT MARNOCH.

Name:—The Congregations of Marnoch and New Marnoch shall be united *new church of marnoch* under the name of "The Church of Marnoch" as from ....

Bounds:—The bounds to be served shall be the bounds of the former Quoad Omnia Parish of Marnoch.

Property and Funds:—The property and funds belonging to each Congregation shall become the property and funds of the united Congregation, and shall be duly transferred to the united Congregation.

Places of Worship:—Regular Services shall be held in both Churches as follows:—

(1) In each month there shall be two morning services in each Church; and two evening services in New Marnoch Church and two evening services in Aberchirder Church Hall.

(2) In the four months having five Sundays in the month two morning services shall be held in New Marnoch Church and two in Marnoch Church, the latter being in the summer months. Two evening services shall be held in Aberchirder Church Hall and two in New Marnoch Church.

Kirk Session:—The Elders of both Congregations shall be the Elders of the united Congregation and shall form, with the Minister, the Kirk Session of the united Congregation.

The Deacons of New Marnoch Congregation shall be invited to become Elders of the united Congregation.

Congregational Management:—The Kirk-Session shall administer the temporal affairs of the united Congregation.

Minister:—The United Congregation shall proceed to the Election and Appointment of a Minister of the united Congregation as soon as the New Marnoch Church shall have been declared Vacant, and the union of the two Congregations shall have been consummated.

Manse:—The Minister of the united Congregation shall reside in Aberchirder, and in the meantime in the present New Marnoch Manse. The present Minister of New Marnoch Church, having resigned to facilitate Union, shall be entitled to reside in Marnoch Church Manse until he shall be transferred to another Charge. Thereafter Marnoch Manse shall be sold, let or otherwise disposed of as the united Congregation shall determine.

Ministerial Support:—The Ministerial Support shall be in accordance with the usual Maintenance of the Ministry Vacancy Schedule.

Power to readjust:—While these articles and terms shall form a basis of Union for the two Congregations now uniting, the United Congregation shall be free to readjust these arrangements, subject to the approval of the Presbytery as need may arise.

Marnoch and New Marnoch remained as two separate congregations till 1953. In the previous year the vacancy at Marnoch had led the Presbytery to propose a union and after lengthy discussions and compromises the two congregations reached agreement.[126, 127] The Rev Strachan assisted negotiations by demitting his charge to fit in with Marnoch's wish to have an entirely new minister elected. The union was marked by a joint service held in New Marnoch Church on 11 January 1953, conducted by the Rev D McRae, Keith.[128]

Services were held in both the old and new churches until 1990, when the last regular service was held in the former. But as Marnoch celebrates its 200th anniversary and New Marnoch its 150th, members of the congregation will feel affection for both the old church, in its beautiful setting above the Deveron, and the new church in Aberchirder, built to accommodate a congregation determined to worship God led by their democratically elected minister, David Henry.

THE CHURCHES AND MANSES IN 1992

The present appearance of New Marnoch Church dates from only 1964, prior to which its walls were harled. When reharling became necessary in that year it was decided that the stonework was so sound and attractive that the walls should be pointed and left exposed. [129]

A similar change in appearance took place at Marnoch Church in 1987 during treatment of problems with damp. Expenditure on this and other repairs at Marnoch totalled £10 000. Although it might seem unfortunate that only three years later the Presbytery decided that the church would no longer be used on a regular basis, the building should now be safely preserved for many years to come.*

The Old Manse of Marnoch, built in 1806 (with an extension - at the right of the illustration on page 6 - added in the 1920s) was the home of the ministers of Marnoch Church until 1953. In October of that year, following the establishment of the joint charge, the manse was declared surplus to requirements, and was sold to Lt-Col. Innes. [130] Since 1986 the Old Manse of Marnoch has been a highly regarded hotel, owned and run by Peter and Keren Carter.

In Aberchirder, although James Henderson's church still stands, his manse** is no longer with us. In April 1957, dry rot was reported in four rooms, and it began to spread quickly. [131] In 1960 a report revealed that a thorough cure would cost as much as building a new manse. [132] Two years later a new manse was costed at £7500, of which £4500 would have to be found outwith existing funds, [133] and most of this was obtained in the form of a £3000 loan from the Church of Scotland and a £1000 grant from the Baird Trust. [134]

There was much discussion on where the new manse should be sited, but eventually in February 1963 it was decided to demolish the existing manse and use the site for the new one. [135] After much delay, the present manse was ready for occupation in July 1965.

---

*   The cost of upkeep of properties is a constant problem for churches today, and New Church of Marnoch is no exception. In the last five years it has been necessary to spend nearly £32 000 on a thorough programme of refurbishment to restore the two churches and the Church Hall to good order, and replacement of the windows of New Marnoch Church is currently being undertaken at an estimated £22 000.
One recent addition to sources of income for the church is its Thrift Shop, which operates in the former Aberchirder Town Council premises at 120 Main Street, bought in 1984 for £4000.

**   See picture on page 17.

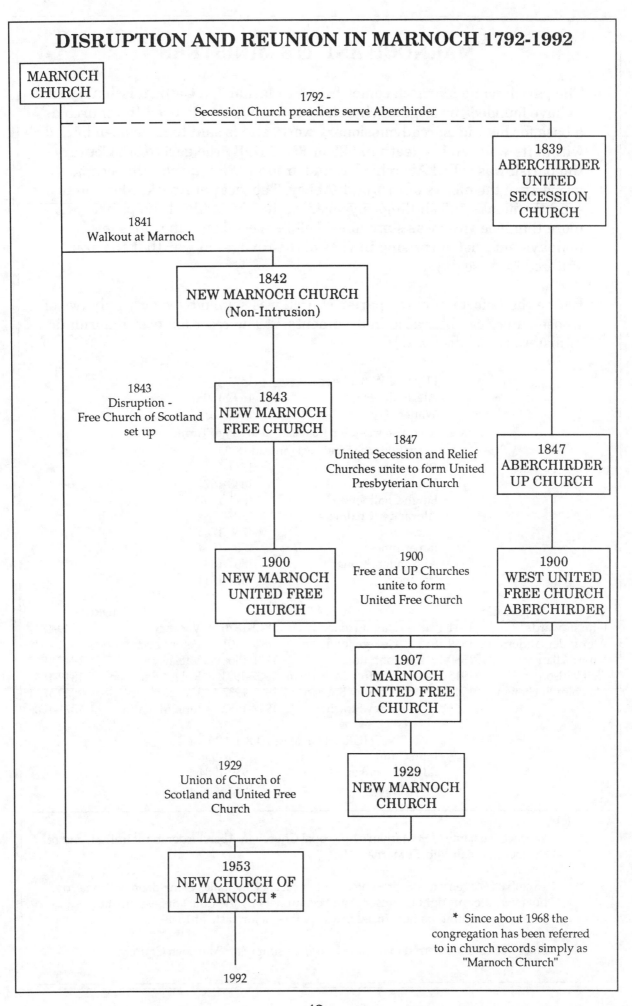

DISRUPTION AND REUNION IN MARNOCH 1792-1992

MARNOCH CHURCH

1792 -
Secession Church preachers serve Aberchirder

1839
ABERCHIRDER UNITED SECESSION CHURCH

1841
Walkout at Marnoch

1842
NEW MARNOCH CHURCH
(Non-Intrusion)

1843
Disruption -
Free Church of Scotland
set up

1843
NEW MARNOCH FREE CHURCH

1847
United Secession and Relief
Churches unite to form United
Presbyterian Church

1847
ABERCHIRDER UP CHURCH

1900
NEW MARNOCH UNITED FREE CHURCH

1900
Free and UP Churches
unite to form
United Free Church

1900
WEST UNITED FREE CHURCH ABERCHIRDER

1907
MARNOCH UNITED FREE CHURCH

1929
Union of Church of
Scotland and United Free
Church

1929
NEW MARNOCH CHURCH

1953
NEW CHURCH OF MARNOCH *

* Since about 1968 the
congregation has been referred
to in church records simply as
"Marnoch Church"

1992

MARNOCH AND ITS MINISTERS

The parish name Marnoch comes from St Marnan*, a Celtic missionary said to have founded the original church by the Deveron. He used the church as a base for his widespread missionary work, and is said to have been buried within its walls on his death in 625 or 655 AD. By the early 13th Century the parish was called Aberchirder, and around 1250 the church became the property of the monks of Arbroath Abbey. The vicar of Aberkerdor had to send the monks 100 shillings a year from the kirklands of the parish, and more than one vicar was summoned before special church courts for nonpayment - not surprising in view of the ravages of war that the area suffered in those days.

Before the Reformation the parish church was served by vicars, only two of whose names can be traced in documents. [136] The recorded post-Reformation ministers of Marnoch are [137] :

Florence Winchester	1574-1597
Alexander Hay	1597-1608
Walter Hay	1608-1631

(Marnoch parish was taken from the Presbytery of Turriff
and added to Strathbogie around 1630.)

Richard Maitland	1631-1647
John Reidford	1648-1671
Hugh Chalmers	1671-1707
Alexander Chalmers	1707-1752
Vacancy**	1752-1755
James Innes	1755-1804
Alexander Stronach	1804-1837
Vacancy	1837-1841

OLD MARNOCH		NEW MARNOCH		UP CHURCH	
John Edwards	1841-1848	David Henry	1842-1870	Vacancy	1839-1844
Alexander Anderson	1849-1880	George Johnston	1870-1901	Peter Landreth	1844-1847
James Allan	1880-1915	John Ross	1901-1906	Vacancy	1847-1849
Neil Wilson	1915-1943	Godfrey McFadyen	1907-1931	Robert Paterson	1849-1869
Malcolm Buchanan	1943-1951	Andrew Buchan	1932-1937	Vacancy	1869-1871
		Percy Strachan	1937-1952	John McRaith	1871-1906

NEW CHURCH OF MARNOCH***	
John Gunn	1953-1958
Edward Walker	1959-1984
Robert Jones	1985-

---

*   Whence the name of St Marnan's Episcopal Church in Aberchirder, built in 1824, and of the local football club, St Marnan's FC.

**   Archibald Stevenson was presented for the vacancy by James Donaldson of Kinnairdy, but even after his right to present had been upheld by the Court of Session, the Presbytery of Strathbogie refused to accept this - a foretaste of 1838!

***   Since about 1968 referred to in church records simply as "Marnoch Church".

CURRENT OFFICE-BEARERS OF
NEW CHURCH OF MARNOCH

(Correct at January 1992.)

KIRK SESSION	CONGREGATIONAL BOARD
James Addison	Robert Bremner
Robert Bremner**	Elizabeth Christie
Elizabeth Ferguson**	Gladys Christie
Annie Hay**	Elizabeth Ferguson
Gordon Hay	Donald Graham
Douglas Heggie	Ruth Graham
Geoffrey McMichael	Carol Gregor
Jean McMichael**	Annie Hay
Richard McKenzie*	William Legge
Alison McKenzie	Elizabeth Legge
Alexander Mackie**	Jean McMichael
Alison Mackie**	Alexander Mackie
George Niven**	Alison Mackie
John Patterson	Robert Milne
Elizabeth Patterson	Neil Mutch
William Rennie**	George Niven
John Stewart	Elma Rennie
Margaret Stewart	William Rennie
James Smith	Alexander Smith
Mary Smith	Mary Smith
Muriel Smith**	Muriel Smith
Phyllis Smart	Nellie Taylor
Nellie Taylor**	Patricia Thomson
Isobel Wilson**	Isobel Wilson
Alexander Wright	

* Session Clerk

** Also members of Congregational Board

LIST OF SOURCES

AJ	*Aberdeen Journal.*
AUPS	Aberchirder UP Church Session minute book.
Banner	*Aberdeen Banner.*
Barclay	Barclay, W. **The Schools And Schoolmasters Of Banffshire.** Banff : Banffshire Journal, 1925.
BC	Aberchirder Bowling Club minute book.
BJ	*Banffshire Journal.*
Brown	Brown, Rev T. **Annals Of The Disruption.** Edinburgh : Macniven & Wallace, 1893.
Corresp	Correspondence re erection of Free Church from 1841.
Cramond	Cramond, W. **The Church Of Marnoch.** Reprint from *Banffshire Journal* 21 & 28 July 1964 for Dr A A Cormack, Donside, Peterculter.
CS	Communication from Mr Clifford Sandison, Aberchirder.
DW	Communication from Dr David Walker, Chief Inspector of Historic Buildings, Historic Scotland.
Fasti	Scott, H. **Fasti Ecclesiae Scoticanae : The Succession Of Ministers In The Church Of Scotland From The Reformation. Vol 6 - Synods Of Aberdeen And Moray.** Edinburgh : Oliver & Boyd, 1926.
FCDC	New Marnoch Free Church Deacons Court minute book.
FCKS	New Marnoch Free Church Kirk Session minute book.
GFB	Gift Fund Book of Free Church of Marnoch from Mr & Mrs Stronach of Ardmeallie, 1885.
HE	*Huntly Express.*
HoF	Minutes of meetings of Heads of Families...
IBC	Indoor Bowling Club minute book.
McKean	McKean, C. **Banff & Buchan : An Illustrated Architectural Guide.** Edinburgh : RIAS/Mainstream 1990.
MJS	**Memoir** (re James Smith of Greenfold) - photocopied extract; author, publisher & date unknown.
MUFCB	Marnoch UF Church Congregational Board minute book.
NCMKS	New Church of Marnoch Kirk Session minute book.
NCMPR	New Church of Marnoch Property Register 1957-64.
NMCB	New Marnoch Church Congregational Board minute book.
NMKS	New Marnoch Church Kirk Session minute book.
PCKS	Marnoch Parish Church Kirk Session minute book.
Small	Small, Rev R. **History Of The Congregations Of The United Presbyterian Church From 1733 To 1900. Vol.1.** Edinburgh: David M Small, 1904.
TSA	Hamilton, H (Ed). **The Third Statistical Account Of Scotland : The County Of Banff.** Glasgow : Collins, 1961.
UPBM	UP Church Board Of Managers & Congregational Meetings minute book.

WD   Communication from Mr William Davidson, Cullen.

Witness   *Edinburgh Witness.*

Wright   Wright, P. **The Birth & Growth Of A Village : The History Of Aberchirder & The Gordon Connection**. 1984.

REFERENCES

1. Brown p22
2. PCKS 12 Oct 1792
3. PCKS 12 Oct 1792
4. PCKS 12 Oct 1792
5. BJ 23 Jun 1891
6. BJ 11 Oct 1870
7. Witness 9 Jan 1841
8. HE 16 Jul 1864
9. HE 16 Oct 1870
10. Banner 23 Jan 1841
11. CS
12. AJ 27 Jan 1841
13. BJ 23 Jun 1891
14. Corresp
15. HoF
16. HoF
17. BJ 11 Oct 1870
18. BJ 23 Jun 1891
19. HE 16 Jul 1864
20. Corresp
21. Corresp
22. Wright p27
23. McKean p22
24. HoF
25. Corresp
26. AJ 14 Apr 1841
27. DW
28. FCDC 4 Oct 1875
29. HE 23 Jul 1864
30. BJ 11 Oct 1870
31. HoF
32. HoF
33. AJ 7 Jul 1841
34. HoF
35. HE 23 Jul 1864
36. Corresp
37. BJ 23 Jun 1891
38. Corresp
39. HoF
40. HE 23 Jul 1864
41. HoF
42. CS
43. Brown p29
44. Brown p48
45. Brown p97
46. Brown p158
47. Brown p350
48. Brown pp292-3
49. Brown pp89-90
50. Brown pp319-20, 325
51. FCKS 15 Jun 1843
52. FCDC 26 Dec 1844
53. MJS
54. FCDC various
55. FCDC 6 Jun 1871
56. HoF
57. FCDC 13 Nov 1844
58. HE 23 Jul 1864
59. FCKS 2 Jul 1843
60. PCKS 4 Apr 1847
61. PCKS 9 May 1847
62. PCKS 6 Apr 1851
63. PCKS 13 Apr 1851
64. PCKS 26 Jul 1851
65. FCKS 14 Nov 1889
66. HoF
67. Barclay p243
68. FCDC 11 Dec 1844
69. Barclay p243
70. Barclay p249
71. Barclay p249
72. FCDC various
73. Barclay p243
74. Barclay p245
75. Barclay pp244-5
76. Barclay pp246-7
77. BJ 26 Oct 1926
78. AJ 3 Feb 1841
79. AJ 3 Feb 1841
80. Corresp
81. Fasti p324
82. PCKS Oct 1848
83. BJ 3 Oct 1848
84. BJ 3 Oct 1848
85. Cramond p12
86. PCKS 18 Apr 1880
87. PCKS 18 Apr 1880
88. BJ 11 Oct 1870
89. HE 16 Jul 1864
90. HE 16 Oct 1870
91. FCKS 9 Nov 1870
92. FCDC 5 Jul 1871
93. HE 27 Jun 1891
94. HE 7 Jan 1893
95. PCKS 12 Sep 1886
96. PCKS 7 Sep 1890
97. HE 8 Apr 1893
98. GFB
99. PCKS 21 Feb 1898
100. PCKS 21 Feb 1898
101. PCKS 1 May 1898
102. PCKS 30 Apr 1899
103. PCKS 4 Dec 1898
104. PCKS 12 May 1901
105. PCKS 23 Aug 1942
106. PCKS 6 Aug 1945
107. IBC 29 Sep 1960
108. BC 22 Feb 1978
109. PCKS 18 Jan 1924
110. Small p127
111. Small p127
112. UPBM 7 Nov 1889
113. BJ 19 Nov 1889
114. Small p127
115. BJ 19 Nov 1889
116. Small p129
117. FCDC 20 Dec 1906
118. MUFCB 1 Nov 1921
119. FCKS 29 Jun 1941
120. BJ 1 Jul 1941
121. NMCB 14 May 1937
122. WD
123. NCMKS 27 Dec 1959
124. CS
125. TSA p297
126. PCKS 17 Nov 1952
127. FCKS 17 Nov 1952
128. NCMKS 11 Jan 1953
129. NCMKS 16 May 1964
130. NCMKS 7 Oct 1953
131. NCMKS 23 Apr 1957
132. NCMKS 10 Oct 1960
133. NCMKS 8 Jan 1962
134. NCMKS 4 Jun 1962
135. NCMKS 17 Feb 1963
136. Cramond pp3-10
137. Fasti pp322-3

POSTSCRIPT

The surest aspect of researching local history is that every question asked produces more questions than answers, and there are always many loose ends and uncertainties.

If readers can challenge, or add to, any of the information in this book, I would be very glad to hear from them.

ILLUSTRATION SOURCES

Cover, title page, pages 6, 19, 27, 28, 31 - Harry Mantell
Page 1 - Bob Peden
Pages 8, 21, 22 - Brown, **Annals Of The Disruption**
Pages 11, 29 - 1st & 2nd Edition 6" OS maps, by kind
    permission of National Library of Scotland
Page 13 - Original document in Corresp
Page 16 - *Aberdeen Journal* 14 Apr 1841
Page 17 - Copy of original litho print
Pages 33, 34 - *Banffshire Journal* 23 Jun 1891, by kind
    permission of British Library
Page 35 - Original programme in FCKS minute book
Page 41 - Original document in NMKS minute book